The Andrew R. Cecil Lectures on Moral Values in a Free Society

established by

The University of Texas at Dallas

Volume XIV

Previous Volumes of the Andrew R. Cecil Lectures
on Moral Values in a Free Society

THE MORALITY OF THE MASS MEDIA

The Morality of the Mass Media

BURL OSBORNE
JOAN KONNER
ELLEN HUME
MICHAEL JANEWAY
ROYCE HANSON
ANDREW R. CECIL

With an Introduction by
ANDREW R. CECIL

Edited by
W. LAWSON TAITTE

The University of Texas at Dallas
1993

Library of Congress Catalog Card Number 93-60441
International Standard Book Number 0-292-71160-3

Distributed by the University of Texas Press,
Box 7819, Austin, Texas 78712

FOREWORD

In 1979 The University of Texas at Dallas established the Andrew R. Cecil Lectures on Moral Values in a Free Society to provide a forum for the discussion of important issues facing our society. Each year since, the University has invited to its campus scholars, businessmen and members of the professions, public officials, and other notable individuals to share their ideas on these issues with the academic community and the general public. In the fourteen years of their existence, the Cecil Lectures have become a valued tradition not only for U.T. Dallas but for the wider community. The distinguished authorities in many fields who have participated in the program have enriched the experience of all those who heard them or read the published proceedings of their lectures. They have enlarged our understanding of the system of moral values on which our country was founded and continues to rest.

The University named this program for Dr. Andrew R. Cecil, its Distinguished Scholar in Residence. During his tenure as President of The Southwestern Legal Foundation, Dr. Cecil's innovative leadership brought that institution into the forefront of continuing legal education in the United States. When he retired from the Foundation as its Chancellor Emeritus, Dr. Cecil was asked by The University of Texas at Dallas to serve as its Distinguished Scholar in Residence, and the Cecil Lectures were instituted. In 1990, the Board of Regents of The University of Texas System established the Andrew R. Cecil Chair of Applied Ethics. It is appropriate that the Lectures and the Chair honor a man who has been concerned throughout his career with the moral foundations of our society and has stressed his belief in the dignity and worth of every individual.

The fourteenth annual series of the Cecil Lectures was conducted on the University's campus on November 9 through 12, 1992. The theme of the 1992 Lectures was "The Morality of the Mass Media." On behalf of U.T. Dallas, I would like to express our gratitude to Mr. Burl Osborne, Dean Joan Konner, Ms. Ellen Hume, Dean Michael Janeway, Dean Royce Hanson, and Dr. Cecil for their willingness to share their ideas and for the outstanding lectures that are preserved in this volume of proceedings.

U.T. Dallas also wishes to express its appreciation to all those who have helped make this program an important part of the life of the University, especially the contributors to the Lectures. Through their support these donors enable us to continue this important project and to publish the proceedings of the series, thus assuring a wide and permanent audience for the ideas the books contain.

I am confident that everyone who reads *The Morality of the Mass Media*, the Andrew R. Cecil Lectures on Moral Values in a Free Society Volume XIV, will be stimulated by the ideas presented in its six essays.

Robert H. Rutford

ROBERT H. RUTFORD, President
The University of Texas at Dallas
March 1993

CONTENTS

INTRODUCTION

by

Andrew R. Cecil

In the eighteenth century, the three freedoms that political writers and philosophers most cared about were the right to vote in free elections, freedom of association, and freedom of the press. Of these three freedoms, freedom of the press has been the most prized because it allows citizens to discuss without hindrance their opinions and ideas, to express themselves, and to compete for public acceptance of their religious, political, social, and economic views.

In 1791, more than two hundred years ago, our Founding Fathers laid down in the forty-five words of the First Amendment principles of liberties that had to be protected for all citizens. The full scope of the liberty guaranteed by the Constitution, however, cannot be found in or limited by the precise terms of the specified guaranties provided here or elsewhere in that document. The term "liberty" is deemed to embrace the right of man to be free in the enjoyment of the faculties with which he has been endowed by his Creator, subject only to such restraints as are necessary for the common welfare. This liberty includes freedom from all substantial arbitrary impositions and purposeless restraints.

The restraints deemed necessary for the general welfare have as their purpose the preservation of those rights and privileges that are admitted to be fundamental to the well-being of the nation at large. Some of the traditional basic truths by which individuals live are self-discipline, perseverance in the face of adversity,

11

honesty, fairness, public spirit, and respect for one's fellowman. History shows us that these are essential virtues that have to be preserved to make a country great.

Two characteristics distinguish one society from another in their attempts to preserve these virtues. The first is how effectively the society uses its ethical reserves to honor learning and knowledge, responsible citizenship and patriotism. The second is how effectively it passes the heritage from the past that has made it great on to future generations.

One of the enduring truths of our culture is the way in which we value and are committed to freedom of expression. No democracy can live and prosper without such a commitment. Although it is frequently pointed out that change takes place constantly in our society, the values of freedom of speech and freedom of the press do not change. They are as valid today as they were two hundred years ago and will remain as true two hundred years from now and years to come after that.

No less valid is the cardinal principle that the press will remain free only as long as it meets its responsibilities. Moral slackness and a preoccupation with sensationalism and rumors abuse and squander the freedom of expression guaranteed by our Constitution.

It is difficult to overestimate the importance of the mass media's maintaining a steadfast, strong sense of moral values. The media are a link between the government, with its policy-making activities, and the governed; between the candidates for political offices and the voter; and between the judiciary and the polity experiencing the impact of the courts' decisions. From the mass media the public learns about the events taking place on the international stage, and our opinions are in large measure formulated by the interpretation or speculation of reporters and commentators. The morality of the mass media is of central importance since the media play a significant part in molding the standards of morality and justice to which the American people try to conform.

The media must accomplish this goal of adhering to a strong sense of moral values in all phases of their activities. Burl Osborne in his lecture "Responsibilities of a Newspaper" reminds us that moral obligations must be discharged in the midst of fulfilling other, more mundane needs in the business of running a newspaper. The pressures of the marketplace have made both these responsibilities—the practical and the moral—more complex.

Mr. Osborne believes that one of the primary services a newspaper can render to the public in this age of instant communications is to sift through the mountain of information that our society produces in order to put it in context. A newspaper must inform and educate, and it must offer more than a single perspective on important events and issues. Journalists must constantly strive for high levels of accuracy and battle to preserve the freedoms promised by the First Amendment.

The press and the other mass media cannot escape the need to apply moral standards accepted by the community. This leads us to the concept of "morality." According to common understanding, the terms "morality" and "morals" refer to the common sense of the community, its sense of decency, propriety, and respect for established ideas and institutions, among other things. In a legal context, Benjamin Cardozo defined the moral standards of the community as the "norm or standard of behavior which struggles to make itself articulate in law." (*Paradoxes of Legal Science*, Columbia University

Press, 1928, pp. 17, 41–42.)

Because of the countless meanings that have been
given to this term, and at the risk of some simplification,
we define morality as the aggregate of rules and principles that relate to man's right or wrong conduct and
prescribe the standards or norms by which man guides
and controls his actions in his dealings with others.

A consideration of the conditions necessary for journalists to fulfill their moral duties leads into a discussion
of the moral traditions that guide them in discharging
their responsibilities. Dean Joan Konner examines these
moral traditions and finds that they are in fact the same
age-old precepts that should guide any human being: the
Ten Commandments, the Golden Rule, and the Golden
Mean. These ideals (or their equivalents in other cultures) are the ultimate sources of moral authority for
journalists as for all other people.

Dean Konner reminds us that journalists have a duty
to examine their actions and decisions by standards far
broader than any professional code of ethics. Every
journalist is a human person answerable to his or her
own deepest instincts of right and wrong. As Dean
Konner points out, it may be difficult to reconcile some
commonly accepted practices of journalists with these
most authentic moral standards.

One area in which the tension between the deepest
standards of our moral consciences and standard contemporary attitudes is highest is the balance between
rights and responsibilities. The emphasis that seven-
teenth- and eighteenth-century philosophers placed on
freedom of conscience gave the individual a new status in
society. A number of new principles protected the individual from being crushed by a tyrannical majority: the
idea that individuals have inalienable rights; rule of law,

which presupposes a higher order of morality that can be invoked against the power of the state; and the axiom that governmental authority must always be kept in check. These principles proclaim that a person is more than a political pawn enjoying only the privileges bestowed on him by the state. They also assert that freedom of conscience is a source of moral power higher than the claims of the state.

The freedom that conscience demands is not, however, absolute. This liberty does not altogether supersede the operation of the principle *salus populi suprema lex est*— the welfare of the people is the highest law. This principle was expressly recognized in the constitutions of many states. These provide that the liberties granted therein should not be so construed as to excuse acts of licentiousness or justify practices inconsistent with the peace or safety of the states.

Peace and the good order of the community must prevail over liberty wherever the community's mental or physical health is affected. This category is a broad one and includes the exclusion of obscenity, the elimination of drug addiction, and the suppression of mail frauds and other schemes. The peace and good order of the community must prevail over granted freedoms whenever the violation of generally accepted moral standards of the community makes a breach of the peace reasonably foreseeable. According to Thomas Jefferson, one of the rightful purposes of civil government is "to interfere when principles break out into overt acts against peace and good order."

Peace and order must also prevail over the freedoms granted to us when the defense of the country is imperiled. The principle of *salus* is not limited to maintaining the well-being of citizens within their own

community but extends to protecting national safety
from exterior aggression.

In her lecture "The News Media and the National
Interest," Ellen Hume examines the power that the
media currently wield in our society. She notes that the
decline of organized political parties and the distrust of
politicians and other public figures have only increased
the influence of newspapers, radio, and television, which
offer the appearance of direct access to candidates, their
personalities, and their ideas.

Ms. Hume, like Dean Konner, addresses the conflict
between commonly accepted ethical practices and higher moral claims. She believes that the narrow definition
of objectivity that has prevailed in journalistic circles
cannot do full justice to the truth. The convention of objectivity can serve as an evasion of a journalist's personal
responsibility for what he or she writes. Given the impact that the media have on our nation and its welfare,
journalists must assume more responsibility for the
effects their work produces.

As a member of an organized society, each individual
surrenders to that society many rights and privileges
that he would be free to exercise in a state of nature. But
he is not presumed to surrender rights recognized as
personal, absolute, and inalienable. Among these rights
is that of personal privacy.

The desire for privacy that we find in individuals in
virtually every society is not distinctively human. Eco-
logical studies have demonstrated that animals in their
need for private space seek periods of seclusion as well as
territorial spacing of individuals in the group. The right
of privacy, as our courts have explained, has its foundations in the instincts of nature. "It is recognized intuitively, consciousness being the witness to prove its exis-

tence." (*Bednarik v. Bednarik*, 16 A. 2d 80, 18 N.J. Misc. 6331 [1940].)

Derived from natural law, the concept of the right of privacy was developed under Roman law and became incorporated into our common law. The person's right "to be let alone" is the foundation of the common law maxim—which is more than a mere epigram—that "every man's home is his castle" and of the constitutional prohibition of unreasonable searches and seizures. The right of every person to be free from the scrutiny of others with respect to his private affairs has been invoked in the most sensitive and emotional issues, to mention only abortion.

Dean Michael Janeway, in his lecture "The Press and Privacy: Rights and Rules," notes that in recent years the media have greatly expanded their willingness to report on areas within the lives of individuals that would previously have been sacrosanct. For all practical purposes, public figures in our society no longer can count on any boundaries past which reporters will not venture in search of a story. The cult of personality and the titillation of gossip can hardly be distinguished now from the issue of a public figure's character.

Dean Janeway finds a vast area of ambiguity in these developments. No one—the public, members of the press, public figures themselves—has any sure sense of where the line demarcating a person's public life from his private life should be drawn. Hardly anyone believes that the government should dictate such guidelines, and a number of circumstances deter the journalistic profession from establishing formal internal codes of ethics in the realm of privacy. Dean Janeway fears that it may take some great scandal or disaster provoked by journalistic insensitivity to this issue to turn the tide back toward more respect for privacy of the individual on the part of the press.

Freedom of speech is not just the province of journalists. It is the right of all Americans and impacts public life directly (as it is exercised by citizens, candidates, and public officials) as well as indirectly (as exercised by the media). The right to vote is one of the highest expressions of freedom of speech. It gives citizens the ability to exercise their powers of choice and to carry out their political wishes. General participation in issues concerning government makes democracy live and function. However, when voters faced by the brutal facts of political life are swayed by emotion, prejudice, or unquestioned preconceptions, their ability to participate intelligently and rationally in creating a government dedicated to serve society is sharply curtailed, if not completely suspended.

The barrage of assertions, alleged facts, and intentional or unintentional persuasions to which the voter is subjected often causes emotions to triumph over reason. The extreme testimony to this fact is the oversimplification of certain issues by labeling them with terms seldom pertinent to the issues but highly favorable or highly unfavorable in connotation. Human weakness, irrationality, and delusion may prevent the use of our freedoms in an objective way.

The great French commentator on American life in the nineteenth century, Alexis de Tocqueville, refers to the agitated passions caused by political campaigns as a "storm":

> "Long before the appointed day arrives, the election becomes the greatest, and one might say the only, affair occupying men's minds. At this time

factions redouble their ardor; then every forced passion that imagination can create in a happy and peaceful country spreads excitement in broad daylight. . . . It is true that as soon as fortune has pronounced, the ardor is dissipated, everything calms down, and the river which momentarily overflowed its banks, falls back to its bed. But was it not astonishing that such a storm could have arisen?" (*Democracy in America*, trans. by George Lawrence, Harper & Row, 1966, pp. 122–123.)

Because of this stormy excitement that spreads during political elections, Tocqueville contends, men of distinction avoid a political career "in which it would be difficult to remain completely themselves or to make any progress without cheapening themselves." (*Id.*, p. 183.) Having described a presidential election "as a moment of national crisis," Tocqueville points out that the principle of reelection of the President "tends to degrade the political morality of the nation and to substitute craft for patriotism." (*Id.*, pp. 122, 124.)

In his lecture "Reading Lips and Biting Sound: The Ethics of Campaign Communications," Dean Royce Hanson examines the use of the media by recent candidates seeking office. He notes that the metaphors of war that have frequently been applied within the political arena have sometimes blinded campaigners from the truth that winning at all costs degrades public life.

Dean Hanson believes that it is possible to wage ethical political campaigns. But the public must learn to recognize which candidates are campaigning ethically and which are not and reward with victory only those who adhere to the highest standards. Finally it is the voters, the citizens, who must set and uphold the moral standards that prevail in our public life.

In our insistence that freedom of the press is essential to the pursuit of truth, we have to admit that there must be some limits to freedom of speech for reasons of security, fair trial, public obscenity, and baseless defamation. In my lecture, "Censorship: Historical Background and Justifiable Forms," I have tried to provide a historical overview of censorship. I have limited my discussion of justified censorship to its constructive effect in preserving national security and in maintaining an orderly administration of justice.

Although as a rule we distrust censors on the general principle of *quis custodies ipsos custodes* (who guards the guardians?), there are necessary forms of censorship that have as their purpose the protection of the welfare of society. In the case of national security, the right of free speech may be outweighed by a public interest in preventing the publication of information that could serve our enemies. The other type of justified censorship discussed in my lecture has for its purpose preventing interference with impartial adjudication. Such impartiality demands conditions providing for calm and orderly court decisions and the condemnation of any coercive utterances directed toward those involved in the pending proceedings.

In conclusion, let me say that the readers of this volume of proceedings will find that in the 1992 Lectures on Moral Values in a Free Society the theme is repeatedly stressed that the freedom of belief which the First Amendment protects from state action includes the right to speak freely, the right to refrain from speaking, and the freedom of the press. These rights are essential components of a broader concept of freedom of thought; there can be no freedom of thought unless ideas can be uttered.

This in turn is a part of a still broader conception of human freedom and dignity. The liberty that encompasses freedom of speech and freedom of the press is a freedom from all restraints except those justly imposed by law. The freedoms discussed in this volume are not license. The interest of society calls for the absence of arbitrary restraint, but not for an immunity from reasonable regulation. Our Constitution does not license any individual to defy or ignore the correlative rights of other individuals or of society.

RESPONSIBILITIES
OF A NEWSPAPER

by

Burl Osborne

Burl Osborne

Burl Osborne, Publisher and Editor of The Dallas Morning
News, *has overall responsibility for the operation of the newspaper, including direct supervision of the news and editorial
departments. He was named Editor of the Year for 1991 by the
National Press Foundation.*

In October 1980, Mr. Osborne joined The Dallas Morning
News *as executive editor, with responsibility for all news
gathering and editing. In 1981 he became vice president and
executive editor, and in 1983 he was named senior vice president and editor. He was named president and editor in 1985
and was elected to the Board of Directors of A.H. Belo Corporation, parent company of* The News, *in 1987. He assumed
his current title in 1991.*

Mr. Osborne came to The Morning News *after 20 years
with the Associated Press, where he was managing editor,
based in New York. As managing editor of the AP, he had
oversight responsibility for the AP news report.*

*A graduate of the Harvard Business School Advanced
Management Program, Mr. Osborne holds a bachelor's degree
in journalism from Marshall University in Huntington, West
Virginia, and a master's degree in business from Long Island
University.*

*He serves as chairman of the Board of Directors of the
American Press Institute and Past President of the American
Society of Newspaper Editors. He is chairman of the Press-
time Advisory Committee of the Newspaper Association of
America and of the Southern Newspaper Publishers Associ-
ation Editorial Committee. He serves as a member of the
Pulitzer Prize Board, of the Advisory Committee of the
Nieman Foundation at Harvard University, and of the
Board of Directors of the Marshall University Yeagar Schol-
ars. He is currently president of The Dallas Morning News
Charities. In 1990 he was named* Adweek *Newspaper Executive of the Year and received the Long Island University Dis-
tinguished Alumni Award.*

RESPONSIBILITIES OF A NEWSPAPER

by

Burl Osborne

I would like to begin by reminding you of a comment from Ross Perot during the first presidential debate of the 1992 campaign, when he said that if someone came to him with a better idea, he would be all ears. If you saw that program and remember the way Mr. Perot cuts his hair and the way he dropped that line, you will know that it was not just a soundbite, but a sight bite as well.

Now I am not equipped to pull that off like he did—my hair is much too long. It has occurred to me, though, that the people in my business, newspapers, might improve themselves with a little more ears and a little less mouth. The lesson here is that we might accomplish more if you talked and I listened, rather than the other way around.

That is unfortunately not the format of this lecture series, however, and so as requested I will try to focus on the responsibilities of newspapers, as they appear from my vantage point. Notwithstanding an often-heard view to the contrary, we do know that we *have* some responsibilities. These are obligations, especially in the public interest area, that other businesses do not always have to the same degree. This is particularly the case in cities such as Dallas, where there is but one large metropolitan paper.

In order to evaluate our performance of these special responsibilities, we must first remember that it is difficult to fulfill moral obligations without meeting some temporal needs along the way. Newspapers are businesses and owe duties quite apart from moral imperatives to their owners, to their employees, and to those with whom they do business. If the bills aren't paid, the presses don't roll. So the predicate for all of our duties is our responsibility to stay in business, and that is why I would like to start with a little history and an assessment of the current business environment for newspapers. As with most things, the results are a mixed bag of good news and bad.

There were 1,586 daily newspapers in the United States in 1991. That is a decline of almost 200 since the period right after World War II. This decline is netted out of an increase of 200 morning newspapers and the disappearance of about 400 afternoon papers. The morning papers tend to have larger circulations and the afternoon papers smaller ones, though afternoon papers account for about two-thirds of the total number of publications. During this forty-five-year period, total daily newspaper circulation has grown by about 10 million, to nearly 61 million, and Sunday circulation has grown almost 20 million, to more than 62 million. Morning papers have doubled their circulation, to 41 million, while evening circulation has dropped by 11 million to just over 19 million in 1991. This shift of circulation away from the evening and toward the morning is what some people call the afternoon syndrome.

Two-thirds of American adults read newspapers on an average weekday, down from 75 percent just twenty years ago. Readership has stabilized in the last couple of years, raising at least the hope that we might grow again.

Most newspapers once were independently owned, but today about three-fourths of daily newspapers are part of groups. The Gannett Company, with eighty-one newspapers, has the largest total circulation, at 6 million.

Thomson Newspapers, with 2.3 million circulation, has the largest number of newspapers with 124. (*The Dallas Morning News* is independently owned and is among the ten or so largest papers, with circulation of just over 500,000 daily and more than 800,000 on Sunday.)

Advertising accounts for about 80 percent of the revenue for most newspapers and last year industrywide totaled just over $30 billion. Newspapers get the largest share of total advertising dollars, 24 percent, and that is just a little ahead of television. The bad news here is that the newspaper share has been dropping for a number of years, while competitors, such as direct mail and television, have been increasing. The potential opportunity is that as television becomes more fragmented and newspaper advertising policies become more standardized, this decline in market share may be reversible.

For consumers, newspapers remain a bargain, with most dailies in the twenty-five- to thirty-five-cent range, and most Sunday papers a dollar or less. There is much less inflation in the price of newspapers than in many other consumer products.

As you know, the number of cities with two or more independent, competitive newspapers has been declining, especially during the past couple of years. The combination of a persistent national recession with continuing mergers, buyouts, and bankruptcies among the country's retailers has been devastating to the newspaper business. Although there has been improvement in 1992, 1991 was a disaster—the worst year for newspaper advertising in three decades.

Layoffs were common, and some papers did not make it at all. These included the *Arkansas Gazette* in Little Rock; the *Hudson Dispatch* in New Jersey; the *Evening Post* in Charleston, South Carolina; the *Knoxville Jour-*

nal; the *Tulsa Tribune*; and, of course, in our city the *Dallas Times Herald*.

In 1980, thirty-seven cities had at least two separately owned newspapers. Today there are fewer than twenty, with more potential bad news ahead. One paper in San Antonio likely will be closed soon, and a strike in Pittsburgh probably will mean the end of one of the newspapers there. For the surviving newspapers in the once-competitive cities, this is good economic news, at least on the surface. It is easy to conclude that surviving newspapers in these new one-paper cities, like Dallas, have monopolies and therefore ought to have a rosy future. Short term, that is the case. For the long term, in my judgment, that definitely is *not* the case.

It is true that more newspapers than ever before are in the position of being the only newspaper in town. It is also true, unfortunately, that some of them have believed and behaved as though they had a monopoly, acting as if their customers had no choice in the matter. That is a dangerously incorrect assumption for anyone in our business to make. It was that sort of monopoly assumption that caused prices of newspapers to skyrocket in the 1980s as the perceived opportunity for very high cash flows attracted capital—and debt—and it left some of those investors high and dry when we fell into a prolonged recession, those cash flows dried up, and the debt could not be serviced.

It is my belief that newspapers, even in one-newspaper cities, *do not* have monopolies. A monopoly exists when you can do what you want without worrying about competitors. The fact is that newspapers run on two things— readership and revenue. And with or without another newspaper in town, plenty of competition exists for both. There are many other ways that potential advertisers can spend their dollars and that potential readers can spend their time and get their information.

For advertising dollars, we have competitors not only in television and direct mail but with magazines and fax-letters and electronic services and billboards and cable TV. The telephone company, with its real monopoly on local exchanges, wants to go after newspaper revenues, particularly in classified advertising, and is about to become another major competitor.

For readership, the competition ranges from the many time pressures on two-earner families to the hours spent watching TV or jogging, not to mention the time spent with other publications. And the barriers to entry into our business are lower. For a few thousand dollars, anyone with a desktop publishing computer can get into the news business.

Our customers vote on us every day with their money and their time. Every day, we have to earn the loyalty of our readers and advertisers. That is a practical obligation that we must fulfill in order to stay in business.

Happily, our moral obligations drive us in the same direction as our more tangible needs to meet the payroll, make the necessary capital investment, and earn a profit for our shareholders. But charting a newspaper's moral course is more complex than constructing its financial plan. It is very hard to reduce principles and values and perceptions to numbers.

The morality of the press has been a contested notion for a long time in this country. Journalists are fond of quoting Thomas Jefferson, who wrote in 1787 that "were it left to me to decide whether we should have a government without newspapers, or newspapers without government, I would not hesitate a moment to prefer the latter." We are not so fond of his comment a little later that "nothing can now be believed which is seen in a newspaper."

A few years afterward, in 1820, John Quincy Adams described journalists as "sort of assassins who sit with loaded blunderbusses at the corner of streets and fire them off for hire or for sport at any passenger they select." There was a similar view of the press in 1863 during the draft riots in New York. Governor Horatio Seymour wrote that "these events were an unmitigated disaster for us all. Commerce was halted, the law defied and the innocent victimized. Unfortunately, the one entirely admirable intent of the mob, to hang Mr. Horace Greeley, the editor of the *Tribune*, from the nearest lamppost, went regrettably unfulfilled."

During the last Texas gubernatorial election, a candidate (one *not* favored with our editorial endorsement) described *The Dallas Morning News* as the "yellow harlot of Texas journalism."

And, as you know, all three of the recent presidential candidates at various times complained about the press: Bill Clinton over stories that he said did not amount to a hill of beans, George Bush with his slogan, "Annoy the Media, Re-elect Bush," and Ross Perot describing reporters variously as "jerks . . . and pathetic."

This is fertile territory for politicians to plow with voters. The Times Mirror Center for the People and the Press surveyed the public on some of these questions in September 1992. Although a majority said they felt the press did a good job overall of covering the campaign, about half said reporters let their own politics influence their coverage. A little over half said the press has too much influence on the outcome of elections. A study in the late 1980s by the American Society of Newspaper Editors showed significant disapproval of the performance of the media, although readers tended to give their own newspapers higher marks than they gave the media in general.

With such ingrained doubts about journalism, we should not assume that the public will readily accept the notion that journalists have title to the moral high ground. Indeed, our standing with the public differs very little from that of the politicians we like to criticize. We have no reason to be overly impressed with ourselves.

In the face of this persistent skepticism, of more difficult economic conditions, of more intense competition, of floods of contradictory information, it would be easy to forget what we started out to do in the first place. Notwithstanding all the static, our principal obligation remains: A newspaper's most important responsibility is to be the honest broker of news, information, and opinion that citizens must have in order to fulfill their own role in a democracy.

This argument may seem quaint in an age when information by the ton inundates us at the speed of light. But that is part of the problem. It is precisely because there is so much information that someone needs to sift through it to find some sense of order and meaning. Having too much information is almost as bad as having too little. We used to worry because the Congress closed many important hearings to the press and the public. The press correctly objected, and finally the Congress relented and opened everything to coverage. But there are hundreds of these hearings, and no one has enough staff to cover all of them. So we had then to solve the new problem of figuring out which ones should be covered and which should not. It is a much better system, but the problems of context and relative importance remain.

The speed at which information moves today is another

complicating factor. A hundred years ago the news was passed along by word of mouth or by the more slowly printed word, taking days or weeks or months to get around the world. Radio and then television shortened the process, and satellites have made it instantaneous. I was reminded the other day that during the Cuban missile crisis, just 30 years ago, it was 12 days before President Kennedy issued a comment about the existence of Soviet missiles in Cuba. Today, it is a long wait if it takes 12 minutes to get a reaction. The Gulf War came to us practically live. Interactive television, where viewers can talk back, is just around the corner.

Politicians are a hardy breed, and they are adapting to these warp-speed communications. The Clinton campaign devised a quick-response team to respond immediately to allegations by other candidates. The ultimate use of this occurred four days before the election, when a Clinton official called President Bush on the air live on the Larry King show on CNN to accuse Mr. Bush of lying about his knowledge of the Iran-Contra matter. That was instant response, whether or not it advanced the quality of presidential campaigning.

Another question for journalists is the emergence of what has come to be called direct democracy. The traditional role of reporters in filtering and shaping the campaigns has begun to be bypassed. The candidates in the recent campaign used everything from Larry King to MTV to the *Today* show to talk directly with voters, and they frequently were absent from television shows where more penetrating questions might be asked.

Ross Perot's notion of a national town meeting struck a chord with many people, however discordant it may have sounded to others. Like them or not, people watched his thirty-minute infomercials, proving that candidates are not required to speak in soundbites.

I think it is a good thing for voters to have a chance to watch candidates in long-form programs where the voters can develop their own sense of the person's character and personality. It is not a good thing, though, to let candidates duck the tough questions or to let important issues go unexamined while we argue about personalities. It will be a shame if we wind up picking our presidents on the basis of how telegenic they are. Ted Koppel and Bill Cosby are terrific on television, but I am not sure that alone qualifies them to be candidates in the next presidential election.

Good or bad, we will see more direct appeals in the future. Newspapers need to figure out now how to adjust to meet this trend, whether it involves presidential campaigns or the local school board.

It seems to me that this trend will intensify the need for adequate context within which voters can understand how these appeals are being made. Ross Perot's long-form infomercials undoubtedly brought another dimension to campaigning. But voters must be passive recipients of messages like these. Someone needs to ask the "yes, but what about the other side" questions. Someone needs to elaborate on the how and why and the results of candidates' appeals. Newspapers can do this, ought to do this, must do this.

Whatever the techniques that are used to reach them, citizens still have *their* responsibility to make informed decisions in a democracy. And they will find the job more difficult, with more information, more contradictions about more complex issues coming at them more quickly.

Regettably, citizens have not been all that interested in the process in recent times. Until 1992, the turnout for presidential elections had been declining for fifty years, to a point where only half the voting-age population turned out for the 1988 election. It is perhaps a positive sign that the turnout for this presidential election increased, to about 55 percent nationwide and 72.5 percent in Texas. This increase was due in part to the intensity of the campaign and to the excitement of having Ross Perot on the ballot.

There are signs, however, that something else may have been involved. A survey after the election by Scripps Howard News Service and Ohio University showed that seven of ten Americans are unhappy with the way the government operates.

Curtis Gans of the Committee for the Study of the American Electorate put it this way: "This was a vote of anger. It was not a vote of faith." If this is true, if people voted out of cynicism and despair, they may not continue to vote in the future. Also not so positive are trends in literacy, in the high school dropout rate, in teen-age pregnancies, in participation in local elections, all working against citizen involvement in democracy.

Nor do I believe it is coincidence that the downward trend in voting paralleled the downward trend in newspaper readership. I would like to think there also is a connection between this year's higher interest in the election and recent improvements in readership.

This environment of change and confusion heightens both the responsibilities and the opportunities for newspapers—if we are willing to step up to the challenges.

There is greater need than ever for newspapers to try to get the story straight; to make sure that competing ideas and opinions are heard; to offer education, as well as entertainment, to readers; to explain issues that are difficult and complex and hard to understand; to be fair and balanced; to bring to the public not only what it wants to know but what it needs to know.

There is greater need than ever for newspapers to look at themselves with a clear eye, to focus more on what our readers perceive we are saying to them and less on what we think we are saying to them. The messages we think we are sending are not always the messages readers are receiving. We may think a photo of a family's grief in the face of tragedy is powerful journalism; our readers may think it is the worst kind of invasion of privacy.

We had a poignant illustration of this recently here in Dallas, and you may be familiar with some of the details. Peggy Railey, the wife of a former prominent minister in Dallas, has been in a coma for five and one-half years, and her husband has been charged with trying to kill her. During this period, Mrs. Railey's condition has not improved. In fact, it has visibly deteriorated. Not long ago, in bringing developments in this tragic story up to date, we published a picture of Mrs. Railey on our front page. A number of readers were very critical of the decision to use the photograph, a decision that was made after carefully considering whether or not the picture was appropriate. You may agree with the criticism that we went over the line, and in a vacuum, so would I.

However, we failed to tell our readers all of the circumstances they needed to know in order to make an informed judgment. What we did not include in the article was the fact that Mrs. Railey's family wanted the photo published, as a way of demonstrating beyond question the awfulness of the crime that had been committed against her. Had the family felt differently, the photograph would not have been taken, much less published. I do not know whether that knowledge would make a difference in your opinion about this, but it made

a compelling difference to us. Our mistake was in not
sharing that context with our readers. That is one responsibility we can do a better job of meeting.

One of the great strengths of a free press is the independence of thought that it permits. No two newspapers
are likely to arrive at the same decision about how things
ought to be done. We must protect that independence,
and that is one reason it is dangerous for me, or anyone,
to offer prescriptions for how everyone else should behave. I have no intention of trying to do that. I do, however, have some modest ideas, none magic or surprising,
that can help to frame our decisions about our moral
obligations.

First, responsibility starts at the top. I have heard
Stanley Marcus, the former chairman of Neiman-Marcus,
when talking about his extraordinary accomplishments
in retailing, say that those who demand quality are likely
to get it. Publishers and editors who demand responsible
journalism are likely to get it.

We must have a staff that is capable of doing the job.
We will have to find highly qualified and motivated
people, create an environment in which they can flour-
ish, and pay them competitively. The newspaper staff of
the future will have to reflect the markets that it hopes
to serve. Diversity must be a fact, not a debate, in the
multicultural world we live in. If our staff is diverse, our
coverage will be diverse. We will need reporters and
editors who continue to learn, who can develop expertise
in the more-complex issues they will be required to explain, and who are motivated to share that knowledge.

We need to play it straight. If we demand accuracy and
balance and fairness and clarity in our journalism, we
are likely to get it. This means we should not be mixing
news with opinion, especially when the opinion is the

reporter's. The "new journalism," which favors us with the conclusions and opinions and pop-psychology analysis of the reporter, is a surefire way to erase any credibility that we have as an honest broker of news and information.

This means we should avoid the use of unnamed sources, especially when the source is accusing and the target has no chance to respond. This cannot always be avoided, but every time we use an unnamed source, our own credibility takes a hit with our readers.

We need to watch out for the "spin doctors," who were everywhere during the presidential campaign. We cannot let them shoot from ambush. We must bring the good with the bad, some solutions along with the problems. We must protect the tone of the newspaper, and remember before we use screaming headlines that we are coming into the house before breakfast.

This means we will have to be more careful about labels. It is far too simplistic in most cases to describe someone merely as "liberal" or "conservative." It is too easy to use "pro-life" or "pro-choice" in talking about the very complex subject of abortion. It is convenient to say "hard on crime" or "soft on crime," but those terms do not cover all the territory.

There is a risk in viewing every question only at its polar extremes. Many of the television shows, like *Crossfire* or *Nightline*, tend to focus only at the edges. Somebody is passionately for something; someone else is passionately against it. Left out of these discussions is the large place in between, where most of us can be found in most cases.

We need to remember to write for readers, for the most part putting the news in the context of their lives, not ours. Unemployment to someone out of work is not a

statistic; it is a question of food on the table. We should
not worry about writing for other journalists or for contest juries, as desirable as Pulitzer Prizes may be. We
must not tell readers what to think, and we should not be
telling them what we think on the news pages. We cannot
assume they understand why we are doing some peculiar
story, like the Peggy Railey example, that seems irra-
tional or immoral to them; we need to explain what we
are doing and why. If the explanation does not fly, then
maybe we are doing the wrong thing.

Consistency counts for a lot, particularly when we can
understand difficult issues and explain, explain, explain. We can do that better than any other medium, and
we ought to.

We should use our opinion pages constructively. One
way to do this is to let people have their say. We need to
make room for letters, lots of letters, and we should not
be defensive when the target of the letters is the newspaper. The op-ed (opinion-editorial) pages are a great
arena for the collision of ideas. This is where we can let
candidates go directly to our audience, without the filter
of a reporter or a rewrite desk. And we can let opponents
do the same thing at the same time, and readers can
judge for themselves. These pages are a place where
there is space to discuss complicated questions in a calm
atmosphere, a place to illuminate the issues, to delineate
the choices.

Editorials themselves can be great tools. Some people
believe the greatest accomplishment of an editorial is to
raise Cain. There is something to that, but not enough.
The greatest use of an editorial is to suggest solutions or
approaches to solutions of common problems, not merely
to harangue.

At least once every four years we get into a discussion

about editorial endorsements and whether we should keep doing them. Some say these endorsements affect the way the news is covered, despite the walls we build between the news and editorial departments. Others believe this risk is outweighed by the benefits of the endorsement process.

I come down on the side of endorsing, not so much because of the highly visible races like president, but for the down-ballot questions about which voters may have done little or no research. We can provide a great service by doing the homework on candidates for the legislature, judgeships, or school boards. Obviously, not everyone agrees with our recommendations, nor should they. One reader returned this year's presidential endorsement editorial with a note that said, "If you run out of toilet paper, please use the enclosed."

Finally, our greatest responsibility as a free press, and yours as free citizens, is to stay free. It is important for us to be self-critical in a constructive way. But each newspaper needs to find its own high ground, voluntarily, free of government censorship, free of government control. We must protect our constitutional rights, especially the First Amendment. In today's environment, it is doubtful that the Bill of Rights could survive a popular vote. That is frightening. If our press is not free, none of us is free. We have to do better.

Not long ago, newspaper editors met in Boston to celebrate the bicentennial of the Bill of Rights. A group of them, wearing their large buttons reading "Celebrate the First," went out to dinner at a place called Cafe Budapest. They were met at the door by the owner, an elegant woman wearing a flowing white gown. Her name, she said, was Dr. Livia Hedda Rev-Kury. She saw the buttons and asked what they meant. Hearing the ex-

planation, she brightened and said, "Oh yes, I love
America and I know all about the First Amendment."

"How is that?" one of the editors asked.

She smiled, then pushed up the sleeve of her gown,
held out her arm, and said softly, "You see, I have these
numbers. . . ."

Dr. Livia Hedda Rev-Kury, survivor of Dachau and
Auschwitz, citizen of America, knows that freedom is
not free; the tattoo on her arm reminds her always that
freedom is purchased at great cost, that we must protect
it at any cost. If we can tattoo this fundamental truth on
our souls, if newspapers can tattoo this message on their
pages, then we—and you—will have met fully our
responsibilities.

MORAL TRADITIONS AS A GUIDELINE FOR JOURNALISTS

by

Joan Konner

Joan Konner

Joan Konner, Dean of the Graduate School of Journalism at Columbia University, holds joint appointments as Publisher of the Columbia Journalism Review *and duPont Professor of Broadcast Journalism.*

Dean Konner has worked in both public and commercial television, producing and writing over 50 documentaries and serving as Executive Producer of several major public affairs series. Her work has been honored by almost every major award for broadcast journalism, including 12 Emmys, the George Foster Peabody Award, and the Alfred I. duPont-Columbia University Award.

As President and Executive Producer of Public Affairs Television Inc., Dean Konner in partnership with Bill Moyers produced Moyers: In Search of the Constitution, God and Politics, The Secret Government, The Constitution in Crisis, *and* Joseph Campbell and the Power of Myth.

A graduate of Sarah Lawrence College and the Columbia Graduate School of Journalism, Dean Konner began her journalism career as a reporter, editorial writer, and columnist for The Record *of Hackensack, New Jersey. During her 12 years as a writer, director, and producer with NBC News, she produced such documentaries as* Danger! Radioactive Waste, Mary Jane Grows Up: Marijuana in the 70s, Of Women and Men, *and* New World Hard Choices: American Foreign Policy 1976.

In 1977, Dean Konner joined WNET/New York as Executive Producer for National Public Affairs Programs, serving as Executive Producer of Bill Moyers' Journal *until 1981. From 1981 until 1984, she was Vice President, Director of Programming, and Executive Producer for WNET/New York's Metropolitan Division.*

Dean Konner serves as a member of the Pulitzer Prize Board and the National Advisory Board of the Freedom Forum Media Center, as a juror for the National Magazine Awards and the Alfred I. duPont-Columbia University Awards, and as a member of the Science Journalism Awards Committee of the General Motors Cancer Research Foundation.

MORAL TRADITIONS
AS A GUIDELINE
FOR JOURNALISTS

by

Joan Konner

"Why can't we all get along?"
Rodney King

Prologue

Here is a letter I received in 1991 from a long-time subscriber to the *Columbia Journalism Review*:

"Dear Ms. Konner,

"I received a form note from you this morning asking me to rejoin the ranks of subscribers. I'm not going to, and I'll tell you why.

"When I first subscribed to CJR, journalism was an honorable field, and CJR reported on it honestly. Today what is called journalism is actually . . . press relations, and CJR plays along and pretends it's real. Journalism that matters isn't done anymore. Journalism today is . . . high-priced guys in suits reporting from air conditioned offices miles from the action. The journalism that is being done is shameful and cowardly, and I don't want to read about it.

"Sincerely,"

This is one reader's perspective on morals and the media, but he is not alone. For many years, public opinion polls have shown that the contract of trust between journal-

ism and the public has been sorely bruised and, quite
possibly, broken.

A recent best-seller, *The Day America Told the Truth*,
took the moral temperature of the United States through
polls and market surveys and reported that most
Americans believe that the country has no moral leadership—not from our political leaders, not from the
church, not from any of our institutions. And worst of all
is the press.

In the season just past of presidential campaign politics, we have heard all the old wine (whine) of journalism
criticism poured into new bottles of today's epithets:
"attack journalism," "feeding frenzy," "merchants of
sleaze," and the most recently minted coin of criticism,
"Annoy the Media" bumper stickers. Vice President Dan
Quayle was among the more polite. He said, "When
journalists talk about the character issue, they ought to
look at themselves in the mirror. Just plain bad journalism is overwhelming good journalism."

At the outset, we should recognize that most of journalism, about 80 percent, has always been vulgar and about
5 percent has been outstanding. Still, we wonder whether
standards of judgment and integrity in general are in
decline. Are journalists and journalism organizations
appealing to ever-lower common denominators of public
taste, to lowlife news in the service of high-life profits,
principles be damned?

That is what we are here to talk about: "The Morality
of the Mass Media." But even as we do, we can ask ourselves, Is there any morality left in the media to talk
about?

In television—I'm a TV type—that would be called
The Tease. Then we would cut to titles filling the screen:
"Moral Traditions as a Guideline for Journalists," under-

scored by inspiring music. I dropped the original sub-title of this talk, "Why Journalists Are Sometimes Holier-Than-Thou," because when I finally got around to writing this paper, I could not remember what I meant by it. Instead, I am using as an epigraph a quote from a defining moment in news in 1992: Rodney King's haunting question, "Why can't we all get along?"

Introduction

When journalists meet to discuss the troubling questions of journalistic ethics and values, most often we talk about the social world we live in together and the external landscape we cover—government, politics, the business of journalism. Or we talk about the law and the principles we live by in a First Amendment society—freedom, responsibility, and the pursuit of truth.

My impulse was to reverse polarity and to talk about the inside, invisible forces that guide journalism, the internal geography of the journalist's mind. Journalists are, after all, individuals, as well as members of domestic, professional, and civic families. We are, before and after our labels, our Selves, capital S.

To me, the umbrella title of this lecture series, "Moral Values in a Free Society," embraces both the inner and the outer worlds. The free society is the external, the civic air we breathe. Values arise from the inner architecture of our experience, our intellectual and psychological processes, and the private forces that motivate our actions.

I want to focus on the point of intersection between the private self and the actor in society, between the journalist as an individual and the community, and on the connecting point of inner values with outer behavior that is the defining point of character, the word about which we heard so much in this presidential election. Character is the bridge between our beliefs and our behavior. Character is the glue of personality, the connective tissue that makes a person whole, integrated, a person of integrity.

The key word is connection, which, after all, is part of the very definition of journalism. As brokers of information and ideas—honest brokers—journalists connect the personal to the public, the individual to the community. When journalists are disconnected from themselves, then all of journalism lacks integrity. As the connection to the community, and an expression of the public mind, journalism without integrity can destroy the character of a nation.

Assumption

Before proceeding, we should examine an implicit assumption: that journalists care about trust and character and that they seek credibility. There is evidence to support that statement. In fact, journalists seemed obsessed with these traits.

Probably no other field has spawned so many codes of ethics as journalism, all in pursuit of trust and credibility. Thousands of news organizations have one. So do the professional associations to which many journalists belong, groups such as the American Society of Newspaper Editors; the Associated Press Managing Editors; and Sigma Delta Chi, the Society of Professional Journalists. Journalism schools can seriously damage their reputation and accreditation if they do not require courses in ethics, a subject that every experienced journalist, it seems, feels qualified to teach.

Two typical examples from different codes of ethics:

"A good newspaper is fair, accurate, honest, responsible, independent and decent." Associated Press Managing Editors.

"We have an obligation to protect the public from all those who would mislead and corrupt." *Muskegon (Michigan) Chronicle.* (That's where holier-than-thou fits in.)

And these others:

"Distinguish your abundant legal rights from your abundant moral responsibility."

"Consistently meet the high moral standards by which you judge others."

Here's a useful one:

"When you write about moral issues, do not moralize."

And finally:

"Let truth be your guiding principle."

If there is no trust between the journalist and the public, then the newspaper or the electronic news organization will find it has no public. Indeed, circulation and ratings are in decline, and it appears that this lack of trust is at least part of the reason. Credibility is the journalist's currency. That is what codes of ethics are about.

But are codes of ethics enough for journalists to secure the moral authority required to fulfill a contract of trust with the public? Wherein lies the moral core for any code of ethics? In the industry? Not likely, when commerce and profits drive choices and decisions. In the profession? The profession has no legal power to impose a code of conduct. In the individual? It depends on the individual.

To find a moral core for journalistic ethics, we have to explore what it is that constitutes moral authority.

Sources of Moral Authority

In all of anthropology, the study of cultures, no society exists where everyone goes around doing what he or she pleases. Without some discipline, there would be no society and no culture. As the Jews said, "Wise restraints make men free."

Something must guide human beings to accept limits on their behavior. Since moral authority does not exist in a vacuum, from what do moral traditions derive their power? Throughout history, we find that moral authority derives from ideals. Idealism is a precondition for any discipline, any code of ethics, any system of morals. The ideal can be God, a hero, an abstract idea, or (for some) a higher self.

Emile Durkheim, the nineteenth-century French sociologist, wrote in *Elementary Forms of Religious Life*: "A society can neither create itself, nor recreate itself, without at the same time creating an ideal. . . . The ideal society is not outside the real society. It is part of it." (The Free Press, 1954, p. 422.) We cannot disagree.

Throughout human history, there has been no more powerful and important force than religion as a way to express ideals. In religion, the authority is vested in God as a personification of the ideal. God is the locus of moral authority, laying out the rules of what ought and ought not to be done. Ethics, the discipline dealing with what is good and bad, is an ordered reflection on morality.

Only in post-Enlightenment Western society was religion's authority challenged and morality subsequently divorced from religion. But even later philosophers, such as Immanuel Kant and others, saw religion and morality as mutually necessary. Kant wrote, "Act only according to that maxim by which you can at the same time will that it should become a universal law." That was known as the categorical imperative, and it refers to an innate awareness of a universal moral law, for which God was considered the source.

In our own history, we sometimes forget that America's authority for statehood was derived from God. The Declaration of Independence and the Constitution took their moral authority and this country's legitimacy from God, not a particular god, but God as an absolute, an ideal. This country was founded as a deist democracy, documented every day by "In God We Trust" on every penny and dollar bill, as well as by our public officials' taking the oath of office with one hand on the Bible as a necessary source of moral authority to make their promises stick.

For believers, religion provides a way to internalize the ideal and, through belief in God, a way to make the ideal part of the self. In that sense, religion is the practice of keeping the ideal in mind. For the secular world of journalism, the focus here is not on faith but on the ideal to be kept in mind.

Journalists vow to pursue the truth, and we see that ideal at work in all our codes of ethics. But in focusing on the rules, we seem to have become disconnected from the sources that inspire and empower them—the sources of moral authority.

My thesis is that in order to regain, or to achieve, the moral authority that the self-appointed guardians of truth, that is, journalists, would seek, we must connect the dual aspects of our world—the internal with the external, the personal with the professional. Moral guidelines for external behavior have little, if any, authority apart from the beliefs and values from which the action flows.

In the library of spiritual literature, there is a rich legacy of moral wisdom that is relevant and useful to journalists as guidelines. I have selected three examples with clear application to our craft: the Ninth Commandment, the Golden Rule, and the Golden Mean. All are so familiar they seem imbedded in our cultural genes, although clearly we have difficulty applying them. What I hope to do is to make a connection—between journalism and moral traditions and between the self and the community, which is what moral traditions, and journalism, are about.

A. Moral Guideline 1: The Ninth Commandment

David Broder wrote, "It is difficult to write about journalistic ethics without sounding like a jerk." I will try not to sound like a jerk. And I will try not to moralize. And I hope that you will "judge not, that ye not be judged."

The Jews introduced to the world the Ten Commandments, which are today the moral foundations of half the world's population. Since the pursuit of truth is the journalist's most fundamental ideal, let us start with the Ninth Commandment. It says, "Thou shalt not bear false witness."

Although moral imperatives vary from culture to culture, from tradition to tradition, and from time to time, the spoken word has been on the agenda of all of them.

In Hinduism: "Untruth results in pain and ignorance."

In Buddhism, the Eightfold Path, which leads to Enlightenment, directs "Right Speech." It says, "Analyze what you say to identify lack of truth."

The Koran says, "Eschew the speaking of falsehood."

Christ said, "A man is defiled not by what goes into his mouth, but by what comes out of it," meaning that untruth defiles the person who utters it.

I think that we, as journalists, have no reasoned argument with that moral tradition as our fundamental guideline, although we seem to have a great deal of difficulty implementing it for a multitude of reasons, only some of which are forgivable. Acceptable reasons for bearing false witness are by reason of honest error or by reason of a limited view or incompleteness. Unacceptable reasons are by reason of ignorance, by reason of haste, by reason of dishonesty, by reason of bias, and by reason of ambition, as in beat the competition at any price for corporate or personal gain.

While we are talking about Right Speech and the Ninth Commandment, here are some other, more popular failings of journalism in this category: tactlessness; disrespect; gossip, although not all of it, as the critics seem to imply; questions asked rudely; rude questions; and sometimes the right question asked at the wrong time. An example of the latter was the question about an unsubstantiated report of an extramarital affair posed to George Bush at a press conference with the leader of another nation following sensitive negotiations.

And can we talk about Right Speech without pausing to consider the problems of language itself? Any writer knows that words fail experience in almost every case. Words and edited pictures by definition create a pseudo- or symbolic world that gets between the writer and the event or between the writer and what the writer meant to say—in short, between the author and the audience. As journalists, we are limited not only by our human failings but also by time, by space, and, most of all, by words.

Walter Lippmann, one of the heroes of journalism, wrote in his book *Public Opinion*, "Great men, even during their lifetime, are usually known to the public only through a fictitious personality." (The Free Press, 1965, p. 5.) Lippmann understood that the creation of a fiction is inevitably part of human communication.

Journalists, in a sense of false humility, like to say we just cover reality, we do not create it; but the reality is we do both. Not only do we cover events, but in so doing, we create a new reality as well. Ask any public person. Recent data in experimental psychology suggest that the reality we regard as "out there" waiting to be discovered is a false notion. A more accurate picture might be that the reality we see is invented by the act of observation. Not only does the observer change the observation, as science tells us, but the observer changes the observed. Not only is seeing believing, but believing is seeing.

Journalists create reality in another sense as well. By our reports, we collectively construct a picture of the world that becomes the cornerstone of public perceptions from which actions and judgments follow. By so doing, journalists are the architects of the future. For example, a bad review by one critic of a restaurant or a play can damage that enterprise and possibly put it out of business. Likewise, a bad review of life, which is, in fact, the prevailing definition of news, can harm society as a whole. Focusing on the negative, reporting mostly when things go wrong, can put the human enterprise out of business, which does not, in fact, appear today to be an impossible or absurd proposition. Such is the negative power of knowledge.

B. *Moral Guideline 2: The Golden Rule*

Another treasure of perennial wisdom with resonance for journalists comes from the Sermon on the Mount: "Do unto others as you would have them do unto you." It is known as the Golden Rule, and it requires empathy, the ability to put yourself in someone else's shoes, a character trait considered subversive for journalists. Empathy would undermine that proud imperative of journalism, objectivity, although columnists and critics— who have the permit, indeed, the privilege, of subjectivity—seem to be the most wanting.

Consider, for example, the epidemic disease of victimizing subjects of news stories, which has been written about in innumerable books, such as Larry Sabato's *Feeding Frenzy* and Suzanne Garment's *Scandal*. Put yourself in Dan Quayle's shoes. Or Bill Clinton's shoes. Or Leona Helmsley's shoes. Or Imelda Marcos's shoes. It is common today to read and see the news media putting citizens in the cross hairs of reporting and commentary and pulling the verbal or visual trigger. Sometimes I think that our school should offer group therapy for journalists who practice "press abuse" and "subject battering," and also provide a twelve-step program for those suffering from "byline addiction." Come to think of it, such programs might easily attract government support.

Like the Ninth Commandment, the Golden Rule has echoes in all moral traditions.

In Hindu doctrine: "Every action performed upon the external world has its correlative internal reaction upon the doer."

From Socrates: "Do not do to others that at which you would be angry if you suffered it yourself."

Aristotle, when asked how we should behave toward our friends, replied, "Exactly as we would they should behave to us."

Confucius gives the maxim expression in his theory of reciprocity: "What you do not like if done to yourself, do not do unto others."

Some people might be tempted to argue that most press victims brought public scorn and contempt upon themselves. Think again. The journalist's mission is to seek, to question, to report, to illuminate, to try to make sense of things, to reveal the abuse of power. By what definition does journalism become the agent of public punishment, a hanging judge—that is, become an abuser of power itself? As the Bible says, "As a man sows, so shall he reap." Are we mirroring the world, or is the world mirroring us?

C. Moral Guideline 3: The Golden Mean

In the news business, we are what we ask. I ask myself, when we draw up codes of ethics, are we asking ourselves the proper questions? Do we ask, how often and how many times can news be repeated without becoming exaggeration, distortion, and hype? How much is enough? How many times can one news organization report Quayle's spelling error or rebroadcast the tape of the beating of Rodney King? Consider the pack, indeed, the mob, of journalists around the Gennifer Flowers story and the Mia Farrow/Woody Allen court case.

For such everyday, common, even creative, editorial decisions that lie at the intersection of idealism and the marketplace, we find in every tradition the moral guideline known as the Golden Mean, calling for moderation in all things.

Aristotle put it this way: "To go too far is as bad as to fall short."

Confucius said simply, "Avoid excess."

The Golden Mean is a guideline for journalists for the variety of editorial decisions involving excess, of which there are far too many in this trade: excess of repetition; excess of compression; excess of skepticism; excess of zeal; even in some cases, you may be surprised to hear me say, excess of principle, as in the invocation of "the public's right to know."

The public's right to know as an absolute principle has evolved over time into not only the journalist's right but the journalist's duty to publish any and all information. The journalist who unfurls that beleaguered banner in defense of every disclosure—from a rape victim's identity without her permission to Arthur Ashe's tragic affliction with the AIDS virus, which he chose to keep private—belies and denies the judgments that go into every editorial decision and every definition of news. Excess pervades the industry, especially an excess of reporting about an excess of trivial stories.

There are no absolutes in news, not even freedom of speech and of the press in this country—sacred perhaps; precious, certainly; but not absolute. When absolutes are invoked, it is more commonly to serve commercial and marketplace values than to serve human or democratic values, or even journalistic values.

The only absolute in terms of publication is an absolute need to choose, to decide. To publish or not to publish, that is the question, and it is not without frequent debate between reporter and editor; editor and publisher; publisher and parent corporation; and the corporation, the community, and the country. In each and every case, the possibility exists that individuals will be in conflict with their own group and sometimes in conflict with themselves.

That brings us full circle, back to the beginning, to make the character connection between the internal and the external, between the journalist in society and the journalist as a Self.

The Concept of Self

The philosopher Henri Bergson posited the coexistence of two selves: the one social, the other fundamental, which he regarded as the authentic self. Bergson wrote that it was the function of the will to recover the fundamental self from not only the requirements of social life in general, but also language in particular, specifically the language ordinarily spoken in which every word already has a social meaning. Bergson regarded our everyday social language as filled with cliches but necessary for communication with others in an external world quite distinct from our selves.

In the book *Working* by Studs Terkel, we find an articulation of that core dilemma for journalists—the conflict within the self. Terkel reports his conversation with Jill Freedman, a news photographer, in her Greenwich village studio. The photographer says:

> "Sometimes it's hard to get started, 'cause I'm always aware of invading privacy. When should you and when shouldn't you? I've gotten pictures of cops beating people. Now they didn't want their pictures taken. That's a different thing. . . . But that guy in My Lai [referring, I suppose, to any of the painful pictures of that Vietnam massacre]— I couldn't have done it." (Pantheon Books, 1974, p. 154.)

Freedman expresses what every journalist must feel at some point on the job, if the journalist is a person of natural human feeling in touch with his or her "inside." Invading privacy is inherent in journalism and is supported by the highest purposes and principles of democracy and the public's right to know. If invasion of privacy in certain situations offends your values as a self, then you are in conflict with your role as a journalist. And if you honor your authentic self and not your self in its public, social role, then you are abdicating your role as journalist—for example, the reporter who rescued a child trying to escape from Bosnia instead of reporting the story.

In searching moral traditions for guidelines, we find the concept of the self as the central point and bedrock of every moral tradition, of every religion and moral philosophy.

"Know thyself," said Socrates, the greatest of intellectual explorers, as he stepped ashore in the new world of Western intellectual and moral ideals. Socrates held that every other pursuit of knowledge was laughable without self-knowledge, and he connected self-knowledge with living a morally right life.

We find earlier expressions of the concept of self in Eastern religions as well. In the Eightfold Path of Buddha, Number 7 is Right Mindfulness: "Overcome ignorance in favor of self-knowledge." Buddha believed that self-knowledge is true knowledge, which is available to all in this lifetime.

If there is a North Star by which to navigate our time on earth and the choices we make, that star is not one fixed point of morality or moral tradition, but the point from which all possibilities flow—good and bad, constructive and destructive, right and wrong. That point is like the center point of a graph, the zero, a neutral point, called the origin by a sublime coincidence of language and symbol. The origin is the nothing, the emptiness in the circle, that is the beginning and the end, a black hole in an uncharted sea of possibilities, the invisible polestar of every action, the point of connection. That star is named the Self, the self we cannot see, the origin of every decision, every choice. The Self is the source.

Imagine that you are a journalist. Your assignment desk gets word of a plane crash in Scotland. The editor dispatches you to the airport where friends and relatives are waiting to greet their loved ones. The flight is Pan Am 103.

Will we who saw it ever erase from our minds the picture of the mother of one of the victims as she fell to the floor at the airport, howling in anguish upon learning of the crash and the death of her daughter? She was a private individual understandably losing control at a moment of awesome grief. Did the picture in newspapers and on television serve some larger public purpose?

I ask you who are reporters and selves: How do you feel when you shoot this picture? How do you feel when you report this story? How do we, as selves, feel when we see it?

Where do you draw the line? Is there any discipline or code to guide you? The only control is self-control. The only discipline is self-discipline. Nobody—not even the journalist's boss or the organization for whom the journalist and the journalist's boss work, and certainly not the competition—can tell the journalist but the journalist him or herself.

What about the paycheck imperative, you might, not unreasonably, ask? There is much to be said on that subject, but it is the self alone, and not the corporation, that must take responsibility for the paycheck journalist. Journalists, no less than other ordinary mortals, face demands, responsibilities, and compromises in life, from inside as well as from outside ourselves. We must make tradeoffs and decisions of degree every day. But if paycheck journalists are what we are, and all we are, then at these professional conferences, or even in the newsroom, let's unmask our pretensions concerning codes of ethics and pursuit of truth. Paycheck journalists do not have moral conflicts, and for the journalist concerned with moral authority, there is always another job, although it is quite possible the next one might not pay as well. That is the core choice and decision, one of the defining questions of character for the journalist.

In the Looking Glass

There is a mirror in the newsroom. The mirror is the news.

Here's a news quiz:

> How does the news reflect not only the reality out there but the inner values of the journalist and journalism?

> What values do journalists serve, the education and enlightenment of people or the profit and perpetuation of a business?

> In a market-driven society, is the news becoming more and more whatever the public buys?

> Are journalists victims of the Stockholm syndrome? Have we fallen in love with our captors—commercial and political interests?

> How do we continue to defend and justify our

habits and conventions, especially our convention-
al definition of news? Good news is not news; bad
news is. The powerful are the most important
people. The meek do not inherit the headlines.

To repeat, are we mirroring the world, or is the world
mirroring us?

Dan Quayle is holding up Socrates' mirror, Buddha's
mirror, Bergson's mirror, for journalists, although it is
possible Quayle did not realize his challenge had so long
a history. With competitiveness as the framework for
business and industry in this country, no less in the news
business than any other; with deadlines as an unquestioned absolute, not in the interest of the pursuit of truth
but of competition—of scoops, profits, and ratings; with
licensing, or any imposed professional code, a violation
of our constitutional rights; with celebrity and success
as cultural idols; with power, status, and money as motive; with marketplace models in which the citizen is
regarded mostly as a consumer and a customer who is
always right; and with profits the lifeblood of the capi-
talist system, what might be more useful in guiding our
decisions is not a code of ethics but rather an ideal from
which moral authority flows. That puts responsibility in
the only place it can be, at the source, with the journalist
as a self. Without a moral core in the journalist, there
will be no integrity and no character in journalism.

Conclusion

In drawing all this to a conclusion, I would like to tell a
story. It was one of my first experiences as executive
producer of *Bill Moyers' Journal,* and it happened on a
twenty-eight-karat day in August 1978 in the Rocky
Mountains outside of Aspen, Colorado. We were filming

an interview with the teacher and philosopher Mortimer Adler. Adler was talking with Bill about Aristotle, the subject of Adler's then most recent book. Adler was discussing why Aristotle's logic and ideas are the basis of all right thinking and the good society, as well as the source of all happiness. This was perhaps not a modest claim, but Adler is not a modest man, as you will see.

At a break in the interview to change rolls of film, I asked Adler a question: "How do you reconcile the difference between Aristotelian logic and the paradoxical logic on which Eastern philosophy and religions are based?"

"Oh, that's easy," Adler responded. "They are wrong."

In our Western philosophical, religious, and scientific traditions, we see the world as opposites in conflict: right and wrong, good and evil, sickness and health, reason and passion, science and superstition, the Self and the Other—other races, other genders, other nationalities and religions. The metaphor of duality plays out in every aspect of our daily lives, in work and family, sports and politics, wealth and poverty, power and powerlessness, even the construct of an internal and an external self. Our language speaks in categories of opposites, and consequently, since we think in our language, opposites have become a habit of thought.

Just look at the world as the news reflects it. We picture the world as a power struggle, a conflict of opposites, a mean-spirited world of winners and losers. We cover mostly the institutions of power: government, business, culture, law. If you are in that win–lose power construct, you are hard news. If you are not part of the power beat, you are a feature or a statistic or no news at all—like children or ideas. Win and lose are the news.

When something does not fit the model, journalists

resist it or mock it or deny it. The news media abhor anything that is different, from Vaclav Havel in the United States Congress speaking of Hegel to the pursuit of spirituality.

Dan Quayle did not invent the cultural divide. It was created by our Western religious, philosophical, and scientific traditions, and it is playing itself out in a civil war in society, between material and spiritual values, between reason and faith, between science and intuition, between quantity and quality, between personal ambition and community good. We are conditioned to see our world as either/or, one in competition with the other.

Albert Gore stands before the American people and says, "The central issue of our time is the environment."

Pat Buchanan stands before the American people and says, "Gore is wrong. The central issue of our time is freedom." (Parenthetically, George Orwell said, "When fascism comes to the world, it will come in the name of freedom.")

Of course, both sides are right. The environment and freedom are both central issues of our time, and both sides fail to the degree they cannot find a point in themselves to contain the truth of the other.

Therein lies an answer to the Rodney King question, "Why can't we all get along?"

This dual construct is our way of seeing, our Western mythology, if you will. Mythology is made up of the stories we tell ourselves to explain our place in the world. Different cultures have different mythologies. In many disciplines of the East, the mythology incorporates opposites in conflict, as two aspects of a single whole. The Chinese Tao, for example, is the symbol of opposites as one, with each part a reflection of the other—the yin and the yang, male and female.

Every mythology is a map, and most mythologies work. That means each mythology, each belief system, is consistent within its culture and provides a structure for the discipline of that society.

In traditional wisdom, all religious disciplines lead to the top of the mountain. It is said that if God had thought there should be one path, He would have made the world that way. God has chosen to do otherwise. In other words, there are many softwares that will work in the computer.

Today, through modern technology, with instantaneous, global, twenty-four-hour communication throughout the world, the journalist's words and pictures connect with millions, sometimes billions, of people every day. Our business has become a manifestation of what mystics and spiritual leaders, from Buddha to Blake, have told us down through the ages: The world is one, one human community. As the phone company says, we are all connected.

We need to expand our thinking. We require a more embracing construct, an awareness that truth is not necessarily either/or. Truth may be either/and. A and not-A, Aristotle notwithstanding. Good and evil. Love and hate. Tragedy and comedy. Ourselves including the Other. Truth is two rights in reflection, both competing with and completing one another, life enfolding life, like a pregnancy.

Conflict is not the only model. The opposite is connection.

Epilogue

With all we have learned in human history, including the great advances of Western science and technology, we still live on the edge of extinction—from the threat of nuclear war to the destruction of the environment. We divorce the economy from ecology, our belief systems from politics, ourselves from our social identities. We go to churches and synagogues on Saturday and Sunday and ignore moral imperatives on Monday.

In the age of sleaze, can we picture the practice of our craft elevated by ideals? Can we conceive of news infused with the wisdom of history and moral traditions? Can we value life, humanity, and community even above objectivity, without contradiction?

Indeed, we not only can picture it, some of us believe we practice it, inspired by those journalists and publishers of the past who endowed journalism with its own moral traditions: Joseph Pulitzer, John S. Knight, William Allen White, Ida Tarbell, Ernie Pyle, Walter Lippmann, Edward R. Murrow. We quote liberally, and often glibly, their visions and ideals, and in so doing, we make ourselves, and we hope others, believe that we are practicing them.

Here is a final quote from Lippmann to encourage that impression. He said, "Those who would make the pursuit of truth their goal should avail themselves of all of it."

There was a postscript to my conversation with Mortimer Adler. After his declaration that all of Eastern philosophy was wrong, he added, "Just try taking a plane from Tokyo to New York based on paradoxical logic."

Wouldn't it be great for journalism if there were scheduled flights to the truth?

THE NEWS MEDIA AND
THE NATIONAL INTEREST

by

Ellen Hume

Ellen Hume

Ellen Hume is Executive Director of the Joan Shorenstein Barone Center on the Press, Politics and Public Policy at the Kennedy School of Government at Harvard University, where she designed, funded, and directed the "Campaign Lessons for '92" project and authored its final report on political press coverage.

Before coming to the Center in 1989, Ms. Hume was a political writer and White House correspondent for the Wall Street Journal *and a regular on* Washington Week in Review *on public television. Previously she was a national reporter for the* Los Angeles Times, *a business and financial reporter for the* Detroit Free Press, *an education reporter for the* Ypsilanti Press, *and public director for KTMS radio in Santa Barbara, California. She has appeared on* CBS Evening News, Meet the Press, The MacNeil-Lehrer Report, *and other news commentary shows.*

Ms. Hume continues to write articles for the Los Angeles Times *and the* New York Times *and serves as moderator and commentator on two Montreal-based public television programs, "World in Review" and "The Editors." She also serves as an Advisory Board member for the* Frontline *documentary program on PBS and for* Radcliffe Quarterly *and* Harvard Review *magazines.*

Ms. Hume received a B.A. in American history and literature from Radcliffe College (Harvard University) and has been awarded an honorary doctorate from Daniel Webster College. She serves as a judge for the Bunting Institute Fellowships and as a board member for Harvard-Epworth Methodist Church.

THE NEWS MEDIA AND
THE NATIONAL INTEREST

by

Ellen Hume

The Role of the News Media
in Setting the National Agenda

The news media are, for better or for worse, our new political bosses. Despite their reduced power in the 1992 presidential campaign, they are shaping both our national culture and our political agenda in ways that were unimaginable when the Founding Fathers set aside the First Amendment to the Constitution to protect the freedom of the press.

As former White House Chief of Staff Donald Regan and others have documented, a large part of the modern President's day is spent trying to manipulate the news media to convey the White House's definition of the national interest. Policymakers not only are preoccupied with steering the news agenda but spend another major part of their day on damage control when their manipulations fail. One well-placed article can change United States policy overnight as *The New York Times*' August 15, 1992, exposé illustrates; it apparently killed the Bush administration's plans for provoking a new confrontation with Iraq during the presidential campaign.

Repeated page one coverage of remote disasters, like the 1992 starvation in Somalia, can embarrass officials into releasing tons of lifesaving supplies from red-tape delays. On the other hand, the savings and loan scandal is just one example proving that press omissions can be as powerful as the stories that are pursued. Politicians are so conditioned to following the journalist's klieg lights that the news media were blamed for the government's slow response to Hurricane Andrew's Florida damage. (See, for example, the page one *Wall Street Journal* article September 10, 1992: "Media's Slow Grasp of Hurricane's Impact Helped Delay Response" by Kevin Goldman and Patrick M. Reilly.)

Journalists' dogged pursuit of their own definition of the national interest can lead to the toppling of national leaders—from Richard Nixon to John Tower and Gary Hart—and can make the difference between political success or failure at home for waging war abroad, as we saw in the U.S. engagements in Vietnam, Grenada, and the Persian Gulf.

At the popular level, news programs claim to tell us what our lives are like. The steady diet of family and gang violence that so dominates local television news has distorted Americans' perceptions of race and crime, as studies by Kathleen Hall Jamieson and others have documented. Many journalists are uncomfortable with this influence. It is a deeply held professional norm that journalists must eschew direct political intervention and remain neutral. This means they avoid anticipating or evaluating what impact they are having on the national agenda, for fear this will bias their work. Yet their influence grows daily.

Why Have Journalists Grown So Influential?

Part of the reason for this influence is that our nation is flooded with unmediated information. People simply do not know where to turn for guidance; there are no voices of authority in our culture that are trusted as they once might have been. For better or for worse, the press corps is the only effective filter left between the public and the propagandist.

Political parties, which used to screen candidates before they emerged into national politics, have been decimated by democratic reforms and the rise of television as an alternate medium for political information. With or without parties, elected officials have less credibility than ever. The term limitations movement is just the latest bit of evidence that the parties are not trusted. Part of this negative reputation is due to media exaggeration; journalists and radio talk show hosts routinely blow out of proportion such events as the House banking scandal and fail to portray in context the issues of congressional pay and travel. Political scandals reverberate more thanks to today's media echo chamber than they did a century ago, when politicians surely were as corrupt, if not more so.

But it certainly is not fair to blame only the media. Equally responsible for today's antigovernment cynicism are political leaders like Ronald Reagan, who say "the government is the problem." Widespread beliefs that welfare programs have done more harm than good and that the government fails every time it tries to help with job training or other programs are now embedded in the nation's image of itself, even though they often do not square with factual studies. (See, for example, my analysis on page one of the *Wall Street Journal*, Sept. 17, 1985, about the inaccuracies in Charles Murray's book, *Losing Ground*.)

The public, equally cynical about the accuracy and disinterestedness of the news media, nonetheless holds high expectations for the role the news media should play in our democracy. Inattention by the major national news organizations to the savings and loan scandals and the Bank of Credit and Commerce fraud was decried as a major failure; people felt it was the journalists' job to blow the whistle on such misconduct. Indeed, the public expects journalists to do far more than they actually are equipped to do. For example, the news media cannot replace the regulators thrown out of business by the anti-regulatory Reagan and Bush administrations during the last decade; they do not have subpoena power to investigate, or legal power to punish, the people who lie to them or break the law.

Nevertheless, pressure is building on news organizations to fill the void left by other institutions that have lost credibility. Religious leaders from Jerry Falwell to Jimmy Swaggart and Jim and Tammy Bakker have stumbled as political and cultural gurus. Sex scandals involving trusted Catholic priests like James Porter and psychiatrists like Boston's Dr. Margaret Bean-Bayog have not helped. Business leaders, also a onetime source of guidance for the culture, are viewed as responsible for a declining economy, and the Wall Street, banking, and defense contracting scandals have deepened skepticism about the quality of their advice. Politically influential lawyers like Clark Clifford have fallen into disrepute. Prominent scientist David Baltimore and others have been mired in research fraud.

Even universities, seemingly the last bastion of unbiased information, have come under attack. The conservatives' complaints that universities are censoring their material for "political correctness," unhappiness over rising tuition costs, scandals about their use of federal research funds, and the government's high-profile antitrust actions on financial aid all have taken a toll. If political, religious, scientific, legal, medical, business, and scholarly leaders all are suspect, it seems these days as if there is no corner of our public life where citizens anticipate ethical behavior in the public interest.

Indeed, the very notion of a common "public interest" fell into disuse during the Reagan-Bush years, as privatization has been the politically correct formula for every problem and every segment of society. We have forgotten that the national interest must represent a common public good rather than simply the narrower interests of those in power.

What Journalists Think They Are Doing: Serving the Public Interest

In the midst of this seeming breakdown of all public interest in favor of private advantage, journalism remains an odd hybrid. It is an institution made up of private-sector, profit-seeking businesses that, in a tradition that stems from the press's special protection in the First Amendment, claims to take the public good as its special responsibility.

> "The public's right to know of events of public importance and interest is the overriding mission of the mass media. The purpose of distributing news and enlightened opinion is to serve the general welfare. Journalists who use their professional status as representatives of the public for selfish or other unworthy motives violate a high trust. . . . Journalists must be free of obligation to any interest other than the public's right to know the truth,"

says the Code of Ethics of the Society of Professional Journalists, Sigma Delta Chi.

The American Society of Newspaper Editors' Statement of Principles is similarly altruistic:

"The primary purpose of gathering and distributing the news and opinion is to serve the general welfare by informing the people and enabling them to make judgments on the issues of the time. Newspapermen and women who abuse the power of their professional role for selfish motives or unworthy purposes are faithless to that public trust. The American press was made free not just to inform or just to serve as a forum for debate, but also to bring an independent scrutiny to bear on the forces of power in the society, including the conduct of official power at all levels of government."

Reporters believe they have a special mandate to do what they do. They tend to see themselves as crusaders, looking out for the public interest in the form of the little guy. Sadly, the little guy does not see it the same way. Journalists are perceived as just another powerful special interest group pursuing its own advantage. Ross Perot and Larry King illustrate how discredited the interconnected political and press Establishment has become. As Margaret Gordon, Dean of the Graduate School of Public Affairs at the University of Washington, told the Freedom Forum Foundation Center during the 1992 primary campaign:

"Recently my colleagues and I organized two focus groups in the Seattle area on the media's coverage of the campaign. What we found is that people are incredibly angry at the media. They think that all the media moguls and journalists have access to massive amounts of information that the public doesn't ever see. Many feel that though journalists are supposed to help the public make sense of the world, they're not doing their job very well. They feel that journalists are not giving them the information they need to make informed decisions about candidates. There's another aspect of our findings: People no longer believe that journalists are operating in the public interest or for the public good. Many of the people we spoke with believe that journalists' decisions are business-motivated ones."

The problem is not just that some journalists at times fail, as other professionals do, to live up to their own ethical and professional standards of behavior. The problem is that this ethical and professional code, designed in another era, may actually be hampering journalists in their efforts to serve the national interest most effectively. This code not only shapes the media agenda too narrowly, but it encourages journalists to stop short of performing their most important function: telling the public what is really going on.

In this paper, I will examine how their ethical code can short-circuit the journalist's efforts to serve the national interest. After looking at other factors that also undermine journalism's potentially positive role in our national culture, I will suggest several new approaches that might better serve the interests of both the press and the public.

The Journalist's Ethic: Objectivity

The heart of this ethical code, the effort to leach the reporter's, editor's, and owners' biases out of the news columns, is known by journalists as "being objective." This is supposed to be the ultimate basis for trusting a news story.

In a most inspiring rendition of this objectivity ideal,

Walter Lippman, in his book *American Inquisitors* described his scientific/journalist hero: "It means that he is ready to let things be what they may be, whether or not he wants them to be that way. It means that he has conquered his desire to have the world justify his prejudices." (Macmillan, 1928, p. 46.)

Columnists and editorial writers are supposed to have opinions, but other journalists—reporters, editors, and producers—are supposed to exercise this Lippmann ideal of professional detachment. (Of course Lippmann himself was deeply involved in politics and was hardly a disinterested observer.) There is no greater sin among journalists than being unobjective or biased. Personal biases are supposed to be checked at the door the day the journalist takes the job.

To be sure, as multitudes of scholars have documented and most journalists themselves acknowledge readily, "objectivity" is impossible to achieve. Some openly defy the ethical code. As publisher Henry Luce, who used *Time* magazine to push his own foreign policy beliefs, once said, "Show me a man who thinks he's objective, and I'll show you a man who's deceiving himself."

But that said, most professional American reporters and editors still try. They pursue what Gaye Tuchman calls the "strategic ritual of objectivity," seeking to represent at least two sides of an issue in order to "balance" the story with opposing views, to ground their story in verified facts, and to quote others instead of their own opinions. European journalists work for papers whose political biases are flaunted, and thus they must win people over by the grace and logic of their arguments rather than by their authority as "neutral observers." But American journalists believe, as Michael Schudson describes in *Discovering the News*, that they "can and should separate facts from values":

> "Facts, in this view, are assertions about the world
> open to independent validation. They stand beyond
> the distorting influences of any individual's per-
> sonal preferences. Values, in this view, are an in-
> dividual's conscious or unconscious preferences
> for what the world should be; they are seen as ulti-
> mately subjective and so without legitimate claim
> on other people. The belief in objectivity is a faith
> in 'facts,' a distrust of 'values,' and a commitment
> to their segregation." (Basic Books, 1978, pp. 5-6.)

Robert Miraldi describes further in his book *Muck-
raking and Objectivity: Journalism's Colliding Traditions* how American-style objectivity is supposed to serve
the public interest in a democracy:

> "The theoretical rationale for the notion of objec-
> tivity is that readers and listeners can best make
> up their minds about public policy issues when
> they are given verifiable 'facts.' These facts are
> delivered by independent, neutral observers—re-
> porters—who provide for the reader competing
> versions of the 'truth'; in short, a 'marketplace'
> where ideas do battle. This marketplace will con-
> tain not only 'ideas,' but also facts, statistics, opin-
> ions, impressions and a whole range of diverse vi-
> sions of society. The diversity will encompass both
> public policy issues and lifestyle questions, the
> political and personal. But the observer who de-
> livers the components of the marketplace will not
> give an opinion about which versions are to be em-
> braced. The citizen makes that choice ... reporters
> do not, at least overtly, determine which version of

truth is correct." (Greenwood Press, 1990, p. 15.)

Journalists who are perceived as unobjective or biased are demoted or fired or, at minimum, held up for embarrassment by their colleagues in professional journals like the *Columbia Journalism Review*. Certainly any journalist seen using his news forum deliberately to influence his own political partisanship, his investments, or his friends is not long for the profession, as *Wall Street Journal* reporter Foster Winans discovered in 1983. This neutrality, elevated over the past century into a professional ethic, was unthinkable in the days of Richard Harding Davis, William Randolph Hearst, and Joseph Pulitzer.

Tuchman, Schudson, and others argue that in trying to be objective the journalist actually is more set on serving his own, rather than the public's, interest: "Objectivity is a set of concrete conventions which persist because they reduce the extent to which reporters themselves can be held responsible for the words they write," Schudson concludes.

Yet that analysis does not give enough credit to the hundreds if not thousands of journalists who sincerely try to approach each story with the professional discipline of an open mind trying to discern what is true. David Yepsen, the influential political reporter for the *Des Moines Register*, goes so far as to decline voting in elections for fear that by making that personal choice, he will turn into a biased political observer. Although this is extreme and atypical, journalists do take seriously the need to put aside their own preferences in their coverage. In some ways what is remarkable is not that they ultimately fail, but that they try so hard at it so much of the time.

Unfortunately, the journalist's ethic is invisible to the very citizens it is supposed to serve and, as practiced, often frustrates the reporter's central mission of informing—and therefore building trust with—the public. An honest check of verifiable "facts" is one of journalism's central and most valuable functions. I am not suggesting that mainstream reporters turn to the 1960s model of the "new journalism," substituting a narcissistic lens for the "objectivity" ideal or turning all journalists into advocates. But the way journalists view objectivity today is far too rigid. Their "strategic ritual of objectivity," as well as other aspects of the journalist's approach to news, must be examined and revised to meet the changing times.

How the Journalist's Ethical Code Backfires

First, let us examine how the attempt to be objective is backfiring today. Ironically, the strategic ritual actually muddies the political discourse that journalists seek to clarify. As practiced, the objectivity ritual:

- Induces them to establish false equations between unequal points, elevating a lesser view or more trivial statistic in order to "balance" a value-laden issue or fact.
- Encourages journalists to hold back from telling the meaning of what they have observed.
- Creates disincentives for discussing issues or values.
- Invites them to duck responsibility for what they convey and discourages them from assessing their own influence before, during, or after they release a story.

Journalists are not encouraged professionally to consider that the very act of selecting facts creates the meaning of those facts. The attempt to do it neutrally simply rewards the unconscious biases of the reporter, editor, or producer rather than the conscious ones. As scientists know perhaps better than anyone else, the selection of facts is predicated by the questions asked; what you know shapes what you can discover.

Contemporary journalism is based on the ultimately false premise that a given shared interpretation—based on a certain set of attitudes and assumptions—represents everyone else's reality. In contemporary American mainstream journalism, the hidden bias often reflects either the upper-middle-class status quo perspective or its mirror opposite, a knee-jerk adversary position. As women and minorities are quick to point out, their lives are not adequately represented in the day-to-day news coverage from mainstream organizations, including coverage of politics and the "national interest." This dislocation between the realities that journalists portray and that news consumers experience has created an enormous credibility gap for the journalists that they ignore at their peril.

As intellectual historian Roger Shattuck has observed, a reporter cannot promise to tell the truth because the perceived truth about a situation depends on the experience, understanding, and point of view of the observer. Instead, a reporter must be judged by his *truthfulness* in telling what he knows, i.e., his faithfulness to expressing what he understands to be accurate and relevant. Objectivity gets in the way of truthfulness because it forces reporters to stop short of telling what they believe to be true. It denies the public a full discussion of the meaning of their leaders' public policy choices. When reporters do try to separate values from facts and stick simply to the facts, they are bound to miss much of the story. Anyone who followed *Washington Post* reporter Lou Cannon's objective coverage of Ronald Reagan's presidency—and then read his evaluative book about the Reagan presidency, *President Reagan: A Role of a Lifetime* (Simon and Schuster, 1991)—will be appalled at how much was left out of the daily journalism that could have been relevant to the democratic process at the time.

America's hunger for values is due not just to their intrinsic importance to our lives or to the loss of values in the breakdown of so many institutions. It is also due in part to the fact that we rarely discuss values in our political discourse; journalists are uncomfortable doing that because it is not easily handled under the objective framework. (Politicians assert values through symbols—flags, family, and war service are among the most popular—but, like journalists, they avoid actually discussing value choices.)

Indeed, the more closely journalists follow the ethical code of the profession to be objective, separating values from facts, the less reporters are likely to convey the context and analysis necessary for the public to grasp the facts. The reporter's discomfort with values, coupled with his attempt to leach out his own instincts and passions from his political coverage, can produce an empty, meaningless shell of information bits. The public discourse reflected this way loses not just its passion but its meaning.

Senator Joseph McCarthy manipulated the press's objectivity ethic in the 1950s, knowing that most reporters would feel they had gone out of bounds in their jobs if they did more than simply repeat what the politician they are covering says. Under this operating procedure, a candidate can get away with lying as long as the public will fall for it. Similarly, when Dwight Eisenhower suffered a heart attack in 1955 and his aides flew to his Denver hospital bed to provide the false impression that he still could perform the duties of office, the press corps knew of the deception and went along with it, according to Russell Baker in *An American in Washington*. As Baker describes it, the objectivity standard forced this charade:

> "Because the tradition of the American newspaper compels it to report with straight face whatever is said by anyone in high office, it was unable to suggest any element of charade in the parade of Cabinet officers to Denver. And so, in a sense, the press was seduced by its own morality." (Alfred A. Knopf, 1961, pp. 81–83.)

If one looks at Edward R. Murrow's two most admired pieces of "journalism" during that era—his challenge to McCarthy and his documentary *Harvest of Shame*, one sees that they are not objective at all—they are highly biased, full of value judgments, and one-sided. They also happened to serve the national interest by telling politically explosive truths that no one else was willing to state.

Murrow and other exceptions aside, the objectivity ethic has been accepted as the professional goal of American journalists for about 100 years. As Michael McGerr in *The Decline of Popular Politics*, Thomas Leonard in *The Power of the Press*, and Michael Schudson in *Discovering the News* all describe, journalistic objectivity became the professional ethic at the end of the nineteenth century as much to serve crass commercial convenience (to appeal to more than the narrow band of partisan papers) as to serve Lippmann's rationalist ideal. Although it probably hit its peak in the 1950s—and certainly the Eisenhower heart attack coverup would not succeed today—the effort to stand back and simply pass on the facts is still central to the modern journalist's ethical code.

In his classic book about the 1972 campaign, *The Boys on the Bus*, Timothy Crouse found Brit Hume, now an ABC correspondent and then a researcher for muckraker Jack Anderson, grousing about objectivity as it was being practiced by his colleagues:

> "Those [reporters] on the [campaign] plane claim that they're trying to be objective. They shouldn't try to be objective, they should try to be honest. And they're not being honest. Their so-called objectivity is just a guise for superficiality . . . they report what one candidate said, then they go and report what the other candidate said with equal credibility. They never get around to finding out if the guy is telling the truth. They just pass the speeches along without trying to confirm the substance of what the candidates are saying. What they pass off as objectivity is just a mindless kind of neutrality." (Random House, 1973, p. 305.)

Sixteen years later, political journalists in 1988 again were objective to a fault; the infamous Boston Harbor, Snoopy in the Tank, and Willie Horton commercials were judged more for their effectiveness than for their veracity. Journalists felt "most comfortable making essentially technical judgments about campaign performance—judgments that [could] be presented as nonpartisan and verified by polls and the judgments of other political professionals," Daniel Hallin observed. ("The

Candidate and the Reporter, Whose Campaign Is It, Anyway?" *Columbia Journalism Review*, Jan./Feb. 1991, p. 46.) Issues were rarely discussed and the coverage was driven by entertaining photo opportunities and soundbites. "Many news organizations treat most policy issues as if they are unimportant or exist in a vacuum separate from the turmoil of the campaign," former *New York Times* reporter John Herbers complained afterwards. "One problem is fear of appearing partisan if an issue is pressed too hard." ("Forcing the Issues," *Nieman Reports*, Spring 1991, pp. 23–24.)

No wonder the Markle Commission found that the Bush campaign ads in 1988 served as a major source of campaign information for many voters. Fortunately, as we will see later in this paper, news organizations redirected their political coverage in 1992 because they realized they had failed miserably in 1988.

The reexamination by political journalists in 1992 remains an anomaly. Indeed, another negative byproduct of the objectivity code is the news media's general failure to evaluate, before or even afterwards, the impact of what they have done. This deliberate distancing had the best of intentions; if one worried about what effect the news item would have, one might be afraid to put out any news at all. Instead journalists tried to be objective by presenting all sides dispassionately and then stepping back to let others deal with the consequences.

That ethic is outdated in today's instant information environment. Having the cameras in the midst of the world's various conflicts can endanger some lives and protect others. Allowing an official to go live on television empowers him to reach the world with his agenda, as Saddam Hussein tried to do on CNN during the 1991

Persian Gulf War. Putting some Chinese students and peasants on live during the 1990 Tiananmen Square uprising led to their imprisonment and, possibly, to their deaths. It is argued, but not yet proven, that the placement of live cameras in parts of Los Angeles during the 1992 riot enhanced the looting and violence in those locations.

Under these circumstances, it is irresponsible of media organizations to ignore the impact they are having on the events they cover. CNN, for example, which has transformed diplomacy and even war, is on the ethical front lines every day as politicians try to get on its air to pursue their own agendas. Yet there is no one at CNN who regularly is assigned to evaluating how these choices should be made and what the impact of these choices has been. These decisions are made, as far as one can tell from talking to CNN officials, ad hoc, on a case-by-case basis. When asked at a Harvard breakfast October 6, 1992, how his network figured out when to put someone on the air, CNN founder Ted Turner said, "We decide on the basis of whether or not what he's going to say is newsworthy." He conceded that his network had been "used" not just by Saddam Hussein but by the U.S. government during the Persian Gulf War when CNN and the other networks had broadcast, over and over again, pictures of "smart bombs" hitting their targets, only a tiny percentage of such bombs actually completed their missions during the war. "So we were used. I admitted it. So what's the difference?" Turner said, shrugging off the issue.

The popular conspiracy theories about why "The Media" do the stories they do fail to comprehend the actual mindlessness of most news decisions. Richard Kaplan, the editor of the *Star* supermarket tabloid that paid Gennifer Flowers for her allegations against Bill Clinton and launched the "feeding frenzy" that some thought might sink his presidential campaign, candidly described at an October 1992 conference by the Shorenstein Barone Center in Washington, D.C., what he thought his role in the democratic process had been:

> "We ran the story. I mean, it was a zoo. I, tell you true, I wish I'd never been born. I'd wish I'd stuck to Cher and Dolly Parton. But, I do think that we played a role in the campaign. . . . It wasn't done on purpose, but the campaign is being waged now, I do believe, on the issues. I think the integrity issue existed and exists. I think the marital fidelity issue existed and exists. Is it the salient issue in the campaign? No, we never said it was. But should it have been dealt with? Yes. Did we do anybody's bidding? Just to put my *Star* credentials over here for a minute. I'm a life-long Democrat. The last thing, the last thing I wanted to do was torpedo Bill Clinton in any way. The last thing I wanted to do was do George Bush's bidding. A mountaineer was asked once why he wanted to climb Mount Everest. And he said, because it is there. Why did I publish the story? Because it was there for a celebrity magazine. . . . I couldn't have made up this year. I really couldn't have. I lived it. I'll be just as glad to see it over." (Conference on "Old Media/New Media; Has Politics Been Changed Forever?" sponsored by Joan Shorenstein Barone Center in Washington, D.C., October 2, 1992.)

Other Problems: Sex, Scoops, and Bad News

At that same conference, Kaplan faulted the "prestige

press" for acting like his celebrity tabloid—and worse. Why have tabloid rumors about sex become so powerful in the national political discourse? Does their disclosure serve the national interest?

It all depends.

Certainly the public has always been interested in scandal and gossip, particularly about its celebrities. Plutarch complained 2,000 years ago that "not only are men in public life held responsible for their public words and actions, but people busy themselves with all their concerns: dinner, love affairs, marriage, amusement."

All along, the press has played a central role in exposing the secrets of political leaders. Yet today the "character cops" seem to have more power to ruin instantly a politician's career. Rumors become facts and the accused is tainted without hope of ever getting his or her reputation back.

There are multiple reasons for this. First is the heighted economic competition among news organizations. Many of them appear to believe that they must reach for the lowest common denominator in order to keep their audiences. They are working to entertain and titillate rather than to inform or spark a substantive debate.

Second, the size and the influence of the press corps have grown exponentially. A mob mentality takes over when 100 or more reporters and technicians are staking out a candidate's home or office, laying siege until the candidate addresses the questions they wish to ask. During such intense feeding frenzies, journalists often lose perspective about the importance of the story they are pursuing. Other news is crowded out.

Additionally, television has changed politics. The most spurious rumor, broadcast on television, reaches around the globe instantly. Politicians, seeing the power of the medium, use it to tar their opponents. Candidates appearing on television are swimming in the gossip/sex culture its programming provides. The Oprah Winfrey and Phil Donahue shows, which routinely explore intimate sexual matters as their normal fare, are now offering candidates to their expectant audiences. It is hard to separate out a political culture from the propaganda/entertainment culture that surrounds it on television.

Furthermore, there are legitimate arguments favoring a closer scrutiny of the political leader's true family values. Reporters felt they let Jack Kennedy off the hook inappropriately and that extramarital affairs do hold clues to the politician's trustworthiness. As CNN reporter Brooks Jackson explained at a Harvard-sponsored conference in 1990:

> "We now have candidate-based campaigns in which it's the person that counts. That's supposed to be a good thing, but is it really? Candidates hire consultants, take polls, tell people what they think the people want to hear, and one of the things the polls will show is that voters pretty much think the politicians are all lying to them. . . . Voters don't believe . . . that the party labels are much help in determining how they're going to act, so what are we left with? What is our politics based on? Well, we're looking for clues to what kind of a person this man or woman is. What will they do in office? Well, if they cheat on their wife, maybe they're going to cheat on us. That becomes one of the few straws of information that we have left to judge our candidates by. I think that's the reason why the press seems so preoccupied by scandal; it's because the public really is looking for clues to character,

having been left with nothing else." (Conference on "School for Scandal: Lessons for Politicians and the Press," sponsored by Joan Shorenstein Barone Center at National Press Club, Washington, D.C., March 29, 1990.)

Thus some personal "character" coverage serves the public interest. Yet today's journalism again is defining its mission too narrowly when it reports on each scandal as if it has found the "silver bullet" that will kill off a candidate. A public figure's character should be systematically evaluated the way politicians evaluate each other. Missouri State Representative Karen McCarthy, vice president of the American Conference of State Legislatures, suggests that the questions asked of each candidate should include:

- Is your word good or do you talk one way and act another?

- Does what you do in private life affect your public performance?

- Do you stand up for your beliefs, go against the public tide or the special interests when you think it is needed for the public good?

- What is your value system?

- Do you use good or bad judgment?

- Are you willing to use your political capital to accomplish something you think is necessary?

Some news organizations worked effectively to apply these tests to candidates in 1992, but many of them were seduced, despite their best intentions at the beginning of the political season, by the Gennifer Flowers question. Without independent corroboration of her story as it unfolded, and knowing she had been paid for it by the tabloid, CNN and local television nonetheless ran her accusatory press conference live as if she were a credible, central issue in the presidential race. *The Boston Globe* and numerous other newspapers led with her story the next day, which means they valued it as the most important thing their readers needed to see that day. When the *New York Times* ran a restrained few paragraphs buried in the paper, it was attacked for being elitist.

Fortunately, the voters/news consumers of New Hampshire cut short the press feeding frenzy that followed; they told reporters and candidates alike on the eve of their primary that they wanted to talk seriously about the economy, not sex scandals, photo ops, or flag waving. Clinton was lucky; in another year the voters might not have been so forgiving. Sex scandals still pack an enormous wallop because mainstream news organizations are willing to drop accuracy and relevance tests and pass on whatever dirt happens across their desks. The voters/audiences seem to want it both ways, the journalists say; they criticize the stories but lap them up at the same time.

The economic imperatives are real, but journalists are reacting in thoughtless panic instead of building strong audiences that will stay with them. It is a profound misjudgment for news organizations to promote *entertaining* people above *informing* them. Journalists are encouraged by their editors and producers to value drama over relevance. This leads them to blow up petty scandals into huge ones and to ignore the important ones because they are too difficult or time-consuming to cover.

Instead, journalists should be figuring out how to make the news *different* from tabloid entertainments in order to preserve their own market niche; they should be accentuating analysis, accuracy, and relevance in order to earn the loyalty of their distracted news consumers. When they compete with a tabloid, the tabloid will inevitably do tabloid entertainment better. News organizations might try instead to go back to what *they* do best: providing reliable and useful information on which citizens can act.

Equally misguided and destructive is the journalist's belief that competition means getting the story *first* above getting it *right*. The old urgency of getting the story first is no longer logical in today's information environment. Getting the scoop first was important in the old days when six newspapers would compete in multiple street editions every day; the hottest new headline would sell the entire newspaper. Today a piece of information is not "owned" by a news organization for more than a millisecond; if it is truly important news, it can be seized and appropriated by all instantly, thanks to cellular phones, wire services, and CNN. In most cases, it is unlikely that anyone but the news professionals themselves remember who had it "first." This is a matter of professional pride and ego rather than of the survival of the news organization. Yet it does more damage than all of the other journalism imperatives put together, because it rushes most stories into the public eye before they are adequately checked and understood by the journalists presenting them.

This is exacerbated because there is no process for correcting a story that gets the facts technically correct but horribly misinterprets them. Watergate reporter Bob Woodward urges that journalists spend more "time against the problem" to ensure that they understand what they are unraveling. His partner Carl Bernstein

observes that journalism is the one institution that in-
sists that all others be open while it remains closed. The
news media need to become more open to alternative
views, values, and priorities before and after news stories
are presented.

Journalists' fluctuating love-hate relationships with
official sources also distort their ability to serve the
public interest. Just as the biases of the journalist remain unexamined under the objectivity code, the manipulation of the journalist by the politician remains
hidden for most news consumers in today's news stories.
Some media analysts argue that journalists do not exercise power in politics and public policy-making; they
simply pass through the messages and agendas of the
real power-wielders, the politicians and propagandists.
It seems clear instead that the journalist-source relationship is a constantly shifting balance of power. The relationship often is too collaborative, on the one hand, or
too combative, on the other, to serve a healthy public
discourse.

Journalists use exclusive news items, or "scoops," from
news sources without identifying in their stories why
the unnamed sources are passing on this information
anonymously. Columnist Jack Anderson has been
credited with the line that he will "protect my sources as
long as what I have *from* them is better than what I have
on them." Journalists protect these private sources and
fail in the process to identify for news consumers what
private agendas are served by the disclosures they provide. They could serve the public much more effectively
by trying harder, even when they must protect the
source's identity, to explain what interests are served by
the stories they generate.

Political operatives, highly sophisticated about the

journalists' common goal of wooing the viewer/reader, have become ever better at packaging entertaining pictures and themes for journalists to use. Michael Deaver, who orchestrated the Reagan campaigns and White House pictures, found that the networks could not resist his pretty and emotionally stirring offerings. "We absolutely thought of ourselves when we got into the national campaigns as producers," Deaver told Bill Moyers. "We tried to create the most entertaining, visually attractive scene to fill that box, so that the cameras from the networks would have to use it. It would be so good that they'd say, 'Boy, this is going to make our show tonight.'" (*Illusions of News: The Public Mind*, Public Broadcasting Service, November 22, 1989.)

This partnership is based on an increasingly common journalist-politician effort to entertain and hook audiences. This was nowhere more obvious than in U.S. network coverage of the 1991 Gulf War. The networks apparently thought it would endear them more to their viewers if they covered "the brave soldiers at the front" in a completely partisan, pro-U.S. government manner as if they were the home team at an away football game; the networks became a family-to-soldier international hookup rather than a group of trained investigators trying to find out what was actually going on with the war. To be sure, these news organizations did complain bitterly about censorship and this was, in fact, difficult to surmount. The logistics of covering the war were extraordinarily difficult, and few reporters had wartime experience. But the network newscasts tended to frame their coverage inappropriately, taking a partisan U.S. point of view. They ran uncritically the government propaganda films of "smart bombs" hitting their targets, which turned out to be completely unrepresentative of what actually happened. They did not treat U.S. officials and soldiers as if they were the subjects of neutral, fact-based news reports. Once the war began, dissent—about policy or the conduct of the war—was absent from most news programs.

Christopher Lasch concludes:

> "What democracy requires is public debate, not information. Of course, it needs information, too, but the kind of information it needs can be generated only by vigorous popular debate. We do not know what we need to know until we ask the right questions, and we can ask the right questions only by subjecting our own ideas about the world to the test of public controversy." ("Journalism, Publicity, and the Lost Art of Argument," *Gannett Center Journal*, Spring 1990, p. 1.)

Is it truly in the national interest to suspend this public discussion because troops are in action? Some would argue yes; I think history teaches us that they are wrong.

Consider, for example, one of the most celebrated and influential "national interest" cases in U.S. journalism history. *New York Times* reporter Tad Szulc wrote a story exposing in advance the pending U.S. invasion of Cuba in 1961. At the request of President Kennedy, the *Times* sanitized the story to remove all references to the planned attack. Ironically, the *Times'* sacrifice backfired. "The Bay of Pigs was a fiasco; Kennedy later told Turner Catledge that he had wished the *Times* had run the story, it might have saved him a disaster," David Halberstam recounts in *The Powers That Be*. (Alfred A. Knopf, 1979, p. 448.)

After the showdown of the Pentagon Papers, when the *Washington Post* and the *New York Times* chose to publish in defiance of the government's claims that doing so would damage the national interest, the news organizations were vindicated and confirmed in their new practice of publishing over the complaints of elected officials. Erwin Griswold, who had been the Solicitor General pursuing in court the Nixon Administration's arguments that the Pentagon Papers' publication would harm national security, concluded a few years ago that the argument had been incorrect and the publication had not harmed the nation.

One might argue, therefore, that a debate about ongoing military policy and tactics is not inappropriate in a democracy. If carried out appropriately in the media, it does not have to undermine morale or send signals to the enemy. If anything, these cases and the Iran-Contra scandal have taught us the dangers of too much secrecy and too little debate.

Given these lessons, it is hardly surprising that the *New York Times* handled reporter Patrick Tyler's story August 15, 1992, quite differently. He determined that the Bush Administration planned to force a new military confrontation with Iraq in order to help the President's flagging reelection effort. That article led the Sunday paper and reportedly caused the White House to abort this effort. (See Jim Thomson, "This Time, the *Times* Saw Fit to Print," *Boston Globe*, August 23, 1992.) The power of this one article confirmed even further for news organizations the idea that politicians often hide behind "national security" arguments to protect their own hides.

When they are not colluding to find the most attractive lures for the citizen/viewers, the reporter and the politician are often at the opposite extreme: locked in combat. As the public often complains, journalists usually err on the side of negativity. Policy flaws and disputes dominate the news accounts. Political courage in policy-making is rarely rewarded or even reflected in journalists' portrayals of the nation's business. Indeed, the news is so fundamentally negative, day in and day out, that it distorts the nation's understanding of itself.

Because it is dramatic and gripping, a crime story will always crowd out a story about people solving problems. On one October 1992 evening in Boston, for example, WBZ-TV led its 6 p.m. newscast with four separate murder stories, most involving people killing friends or members of their own families, with no analysis or context to explain why these were "news" to the broader public. The viewer was left with no analysis or public policy issue on which to act—only a depressing sense of violence and insecurity that was augmented when the subsequent network news led off with genocide in Bosnia, followed by candidate character attacks from the campaign trail.

The reason for this negative framework—about governance and the very fabric of our lives—is not just drama but cynicism. The news was much more upbeat in the 1940s and 1950s when the nation's political leaders were treated by the journalists with deference and respect. What changed everything were the lies of Watergate, the Vietnam War, the Iran-Contra scandal, and Iraqgate. Now journalists are locked into the negative assumption that the government and political leaders are lying much of the time. A constantly cynical framework used by reporters covering government and politics doubtlessly feeds the public's cynicism and distrust of its political leadership—and of the piranha press corps that seems willing to devour anyone, at any time, for frivolous infractions as well as for serious ones.

Even though journalism's adversarial stance is more than justified by the history of official lies and the reluctance of politicians to publicly discuss difficult policy matters, journalists make a fundamental mistake when they shrug off public complaints about too much "bad news." What is needed is not cynicism but skepticism. There is a difference. And what is needed more than ever is a more comprehensive kind of news coverage to balance the current negative and trivialized picture of our national life.

Contemporary news coverage provides no comparable amount of serious positive news (as opposed to frivolous, meaningless features) to balance out the legitimate negative news. There is no natural place in the news for positive stories about how people are trying in good faith to make democracy work. To journalists, that smacks of "boosterism," which went out with the Pulitzer-Hearst self-interest crowd. Before a reordering of journalists' priorities can work, they have to stop worrying so much about the chump factor. They are paranoid about being duped by "good guys" who turn out to be bad. It is far easier to write something negative than it is to take a chance and write something positive. One seems in the latter case to be "promoting" the subject of the story, which reporters feel takes them down that slippery road away from objectivity toward bias. Listen, for example, to how *Washington Post* reporter Paul Taylor thoughtfully describes his skeptical approach toward politicians:

> "I suffer from 'fear of flacking,' a common occupational disorder. Once a reporter ventures beyond the neutral zone of objectivity into the netherworld of approbation, he makes an almost tactile investment in the subject of his praise. By morning, tons

of newsprint (seventy-five tons in the case of the *Washington Post*) will convey his judgment to millions of readers. It's risky. Suppose the ingrate embezzles the orphans' fund next Tuesday. Then who looks like a fool?" (*See How They Run: Electing the President in an Age of Mediaocracy*, Alfred A. Knopf, 1990, p. 26.)

The problem with our national journalism, then, is not just hidden bias, reluctance to take responsibility for the impact of the news, the taste for scandals, dissent at wartime, collusion, and combat with sources or the leaking of secrets. The problem, it appears, is that as we lean on the news media to shape and deliver our national political culture, they have not accepted that role with any thoughtfulness. Instead, the news is spewed out willy-nilly, without proportion or context. Roller-coaster coverage of government and its leaders, from the extremes of Gulf War boosterism on the one hand to the snarling hostility of a press feeding frenzy on the other, makes it difficult for citizen to obtain an objective or fair picture to act on.

To some, this situation is inevitable. As Thomas Patterson says, "They are in the news business, not the political business, and, as a result, their norms and imperatives are not those required for the effective organization of electoral coalitions and debate." ("The Press and its Missed Assignment," *The Elections of 1988*, ed. Michael Nelson, *Congressional Quarterly*, 1989, p. 107.)

But does it *have* to be this way? I do not think so. Indeed, it appears that the very survival of journalism depends on approaching it differently.

Conclusion: How the News Media Could Better Serve the National Interest

How are we to establish, then, a new journalism that better serves the public interest and the competitive needs of news organizations?

Journalism will survive only if it establishes a more valuable and clearly defined mission: *to inform with reliable information.* A more elastic definition of objectivity was employed during the 1992 elections and has shown the way for improved coverage in the future. It is a model of more activist news media, which, while they continue to seek facts as neutrally and disinterestedly as possible, also are more open, candid, and comprehensive about the values and facts they represent.

Determined not to be as manipulated or as trivial as they were in 1988, many mainstream news organizations changed from insider journalism to voter- and research-driven journalism. Among the innovators in 1992 were CNN, ABC, WFAA in Dallas, KVUE in Austin, the *Wichita Eagle,* and the *Charlotte Observer.* The *Charlotte Observer* convened town hall meetings, learned what issues were on the voters' minds, ran in-depth articles analyzing those challenges, and gave voice to local voters for serious analysis throughout the campaign coverage. CNN and other television news organizations worked to analyze campaign ads without passing through their subliminal messages and distortions.

These news organizations decided to help shape the political discourse in a thoughtful and responsible way, rather than simply to allow the news values of objectivity, entertainment, and scoops to determine hit or miss what they produced. They redefined objectivity to include analysis and context. Television broadcasters declined to simply "wallpaper" their television newscasts with pretty campaign photo ops provided by the candidates, as they had done four years before. They chose instead to use campaign stops as news pegs for their own analytical pieces on the candidates' records. Displaying less fear of bias and more courage about trying to evaluate the information they were passing on, news organizations decided this time they would call a lie a lie in analyzing campaign advertisements.

The voters seemed to like the "new journalism" of 1992. Part of this was because they had more voice in the coverage, thanks to the proliferation of town hall meetings and focus groups, polls that gave more than just horserace information, and greater access to the candidates thorough nonjournalist entertainment and talk show programming. As the October 15, 1992, voter-question debate format illustrated even further, the voters did more in 1992 to set the campaign agenda than either the press or the candidates. Indeed, the voters deserve much of the credit for this "new journalism"; they were demanding in 1992 that journalists provide serious issue coverage and more complete access to what the candidates were saying.

At the same time, of course, candidates were bypassing journalists and gaining direct access to voters through such entertainment programs as the Larry King, Arsenio Hall, and Don Imos shows. This liberated the candidates to talk more freely than they did in the journalist-mediated, soundbite culture of 1988. But it also liberated the journalists, who now devoted themselves to checking the quality of what the candidates said. Both trends allowed the voters to better evaluate for themselves the different candidates and issues. Not only could they see the candidates amply enough to gain a truer impression, but they were armed, thanks to the journalists, with a relatively neutral analysis of the facts and distortions in the discussions they had seen.

Objectivity, when practiced as it was in the new "ad watch" boxes, meant fairness rather than 1988's precise balance of negative comments among all of the different candidates. When one campaign attacked another, it was identified as the attacker and the other as the defender, rather than being described, as was often the case in 1988, as "mudslinging by both sides."

This is not to say that the 1992 coverage was without problems. The political news cycle remained a roller coaster rather than a fair and consistent approach to each candidate. (Journalists searching for dramatic stories hyped Ross Perot and then tried to sink him; if he had not withdrawn from the race during the summer, he would have drowned in negative press stories. News organizations anointed Bill Clinton too early after trying to kill him off with Gennifer Flowers' allegations. Some of the nation's best investigative reporters went off the deep end chasing stories without weighing their relevance or truly grasping their meaning, from Clinton's sex life and his wife's law firm fees to George Bush's own purported mistress. Too little time was spent following the money in the Bush and Clinton campaigns, with the exception of the *Wall Street Journal*'s excellent investigative work. Network producers and reporters and editors at papers like the *New York Times* and the *Boston Globe* failed to discipline their pro-Clinton, pro-change biases, and the result was that these unconscious biases shone through repeatedly, framing the political coverage as anti-Bush. It looked as if reporters were making up for 1988, when they gave the Bush campaign a free ride, allowing themselves to become the theatrical vil-

lains for that campaign's manipulative and at times dis-
honest presentations.)

The *Charlotte Observer*'s attempt to take more responsibility for the public discourse is a beacon for other
news organizations to follow. Its reporters diluted their
hidden biases by opening up the news to their readers'
voices. They abandoned their mindless neutrality and
detachment in order to help set the political agenda.
They offered thoughtful research and analysis instead of
rumor and titillation. Others should carry this further
and apply these ideas to covering our national life
beyond the campaign setting.

Values cannot be separated from facts, and therefore
they must be discussed in news stories. Journalists
should disclose as much as possible the limits of the
information they have and the spin of the sources they
have used. They should stop establishing false "balance,"
equating falsehoods and truths because someone else is
supposed to figure out the difference. While being fair
and open-minded, they should not be afraid of the meaning they discern from the facts they are disclosing.
Accuracy not just of facts but of interpretation should be
paramount; speed and entertainment should be
secondary.

News organizations could find ways to educate the
public about how journalists operate and how news
choices are made. They could discuss regularly in print
and over the air how their own news staffs operate and
what their own personal backgrounds are. They could
invite the public to open houses where journalists discuss
their work. They could lobby for schools to teach more
effectively about evaluating journalism and its role in
politics and public policy.

Perhaps most important of all, news organizations

need to find ways to write about problem solving as well as problems. They should take responsibility for the environment they are creating, assessing their own impact and deliberately creating a more balanced and meaningful news product. They might even go as far as the Columbus, Georgia, *Ledger Enquirer*, which a few years ago augmented its six-part series about the challenges facing the community by organizing a town meeting and follow-up barbecues that ultimately evolved into a citizens' movement.

It seems logical that if journalism is going to survive as something different from propaganda, fiction, or advertising—if it is going to serve its own market needs as well as the public interest—it must provide more reliable information than the tabloids. It must talk about why crime is occurring when and where it is occurring, rather than simply recording the latest murders with all their titillating details. It must listen to, and include in news coverage, a range of voices from the community who are not just a narrow band of "leaders." It must arm its readers and viewers with carefully checked information and analysis rather than just amusements and gore.

It must build trust in its product.

Instead of burying stories about awards for seven of the community's unsung heroes on page 53, as the *Boston Globe* did on October 22, news organizations can highlight these individuals who are making democracy, community—and the national interest—work. Instead of sending investigative teams only to identify the problems we face, news organizations could give equal time and attention to conveying the problem solving that is going on all around us. The story of how Kansas City banded together to clean up its contaminated Gilbert-Mosley area is a classic news item that will not make it very far in today's negative news chain. You will not hear much either about Humanitas, the new multidisciplinary academic program offered at thirty-seven Los Angeles high schools that is successfully engaging thousands of minorities and underprivileged students who might otherwise have dropped out of school. You will not get page one national coverage about Washington state's in-, dustrial insurance reform, which has provided 1.3 million workers with a quality medical care program that is running a surplus rather than a deficit. You will hear about 100 grisly inner-city murders before you will hear about Robin Cannon, the black Los Angeles citizen who has organized her low-income community to promote recycling as an alternative to a hazardous trash conversion project that would have devastated the neighborhood.

Solutions to the nation's problems are all around us, being risked every day. We do not learn from these successes—or from the failures of those that do not work—because we do not hear about what is being tried.

The old news values—a detachment and superficial objectivity that corrode truthfulness and relevance, an outdated sense of competition based on getting it first rather than getting it right, an erroneous belief that news organizations will keep their audiences by competing with tabloids on tabloid terms, and a reluctance to face the responsibilities of their own power in serving the public interest—will not do for the future if news organizations, or the democracy they require, are to survive.

Vaclav Havel laid out a challenge to politicians and journalists alike in his February 4, 1992, address to the World Economic Forum in Davos, Switzerland:

> "Things must once more be given a chance to present themselves as they are, to be perceived in their

individuality. We must see the pluralism of the world, and not bind it by seeking common denominators or reducing everything to a single common equation. We must try harder to understand than to explain. . . . A politician must become a person again, someone who trusts not only a scientific representation and analysis of the world, but also the world itself. He must believe not only in sociological statistics but also in real people. He must trust not only an objective interpretation of reality, but also his own soul; not only an adopted ideology but also his own thoughts; not only the summary reports he receives each morning, but also his own feeling."

Finally, if the political journalists who were able to rethink their news values effectively in 1992 wish to better serve the public interest as they go on to cover the world following the election, they may find a useful guide in Robert Reich's description of the public servant, as expressed in *The Power of Public Ideas*:

"In our revised philosophy of policy making, ideas about what is good for society occupy a more prominent position. The core responsibility of those who deal in public policy—elected officials, administrators, policy analysts—is not simply to discover as objectively as possible what people want for themselves and then to determine and implement the best means of satisfying those wants. It is also to provide the public with alternative visions of what is desirable and possible, to stimulate deliberation about them, provoke a reexaminations of premises and values, and thus to broaden the range of potential responses and deepen society's

understanding of itself." (Harvard University
Press, 1990, pp. 3-4.)

THE PRESS AND PRIVACY: RIGHTS AND RULES

by

Michael Janeway

Michael C. Janeway

Michael C. Janeway has been Professor of Journalism and Dean of the Medill School of Journalism at Northwestern University since September 1, 1989.

Dean Janeway began his career in journalism in 1963 as a feature reporter for Newsday *and in 1964 as a reporter-writer for* Newsweek. *After working as associate editor of* The New Leader *in 1965–66, he began an eleven-year association with* The Atlantic Monthly, *where he eventually became executive editor.*

In the Carter administration, Dean Janeway served as special assistant to Secretary of State Cyrus Vance. In 1978 he was named editor of The Boston Globe Magazine. *Later he was editor of "War and Peace in the Nuclear Age," a special section of* The Boston Globe *that in 1983 received the Pulitzer Prize for National Reporting. He became editor of the newspaper in 1985 and executive editor of the Trade and Reference Division of Houghton Mifflin Co. in 1987.*

At Harvard University, Dean Janeway has served as an associate of the Charles Warren Center for Studies in American History, a fellow of the Institute of Politics at the John F. Kennedy School of Government, and a senior associate of the Joan Shorenstein Barone Center on the Press, Politics and Public Policy. He is a member of the board of directors of the Chicago Educational Television Association (CETA), which owns and operates WTTW-TV and WFMT-FM in Chicago.

Dean Janeway received a B.A. from Harvard University in 1962 and was awarded a Shaw Travelling Fellowship at Harvard in 1962–63.

THE PRESS AND PRIVACY: RIGHTS AND RULES

by

Michael Janeway

Seven Types of Ambiguity

For those in newsrooms trying to make sense of the boundaries and rules governing privacy, a compass is wanting. Every new case—Bill Clinton's is the most recent—prompts another round of agonizing in newsrooms, in op-ed and think pieces, about what is public and what is private, about what is news and what is intrusiveness and prurience.

"We are moving these days into areas of great uncertainty," wrote *New York Times* columnist Anna Quindlen, deploring the journalism that led to disclosure of Arthur Ashe's AIDS condition last winter: "We are making a lot of this up as we go along."

But as we saw last winter in the case of Governor Clinton, such newsroom deliberation can be quaintly beside the point and overtaken by events. If some elite newspapers show restraint with a questionable story or a public figure's privacy, as they tried to in the matter of the Governor and Gennifer Flowers, others—particularly television news, plus a whole range of brash, or trash, alternative media—fill the space. The candidate must respond, and the frenzy commences. Thus, situational ethics are debated in the newsroom while, outside the building, the beast is loose in a field of anarchy.

Why is the press so confused about the boundaries of privacy? It might help to count the ways. What we have,

to borrow from William Empson's critical study of poetic form, are at least *seven types of ambiguity* about
privacy and the press.

My list:

1. The conflict in the *law* in this country between
    freedom of expression and the right to privacy.
    Within newsrooms, this becomes a question of
    what is, and is not, newsworthy.

2. The *public's* ambivalence about the press. Again
    and again the most careful of polls will record, at
    one and the same time, public opinion applauding
    the press for its watchdog role and condemning it
    for abuse of that power—condemning it, in partic-
    ular, for intruding into the private lives of others.

3. The *press's* ambivalence about whether to stick to
    "the issues" in covering politics, about how to re-
    spond to leaks from one political camp against an
    opponent, and about how to react to competition
    from other news organizations when deciding
    whether to run questionable stories. Is the press
    the responsible gatekeeper for what is newsworthy
    about those it covers? That is what one faction in a
    newsroom debating whether to publish a question-
    able story will argue. The opposing faction will
    contend that this is an elitist attitude, constituting
    censorship of what is all over the newsroom, but
    withheld from readers and viewers.

4. *Investigative journalism's* own ambiguity as to
    whether ends justify means in pursuit of stories.
    What governs investigative journalism's culture
    (echoing that of prosecuting attorneys) is its heroic
    self-image in pursuit of powerful bad guys, almost
    by definition skilled at obfuscation and evasion.

Those bad guys can often be exposed only by means of unorthodox reporting that penetrates secrecy, and sometimes privacy. Standard practice for the rest of the newsróom tends to be less buccaneering, giving less rise to questions of whether ends justify means.

5. Public officials' ambivalence about what is loosely called the *character issue*. Many candidates run on it and claim themselves exponents of "family values" as well. If that, rather than the difficult issues confronting the nation, is their chosen ground, they invite the scrutiny they complain about. An additional ambiguity of the character issue is the question whether sexual or other private behavior is an accurate index of a public official's worth.

6. The ambiguity of what is, until revealed, *secret*: Is a secret that which is private, intimate, and *sacred*, and truly privileged and properly protected? Or that which, suggesting deceit, is *profane* and invites the cleansing process of revelation?

7. An ambiguity about the *culture* and *community* in which these issues play out: Our culture is ambivalent about whether it values openness, frankness, a freeing of old inhibitions, over the value of privacy, the notion of being able to keep to oneself. We will lean one way when the subject of controversy is a presidential candidate, another way when the subject is a community leader who lives in the neighborhood, or a relative or friend. Indeed, an effort to generalize conclusively about this aspect of national character brings one back to the beginning of a list like this one, to a stream

of consciousness in which these and other ambiguities are constantly in question, constantly in motion: a dog biting its tail.

Signs of the Times

Here are three headlines from *The New York Times*
this year: on an analytic news story: *News Media Sharply Divided on When Right to Know Becomes Intrusion*, on
a "News of the Week in Review" roundup during the
presidential primaries: *What Can Candidates Expect
to Keep Private?*; and on an op-ed piece in the wake of
Bill and Hillary Clinton's appearance on *60 Minutes*
early in the campaign year by *Times* columnist Leslie
Gelb: *Journalistic Cannibals*.

There seems to be a problem. It comes and goes by
many names: "post-Watergate morality," "character issue," "feeding frenzy," "scandal machine," journalistic
license, legal confusion. Since the Supreme Court's epic
decision in *Times v. Sullivan* in 1964, there has been little
question about the press's *right* to speak about public
figures with minimum penalty. But the *rules* that govern journalistic standards and practice have never been
so uncertain.

In the media stone age, the great men of government
and the great men of the Washington press corps did
business about the great issues of the day in an atmosphere of trust, which precluded press concern with
public officials' occasional alcoholism or adultery.
Washington journalists did not poke into the private
lives of those they covered not least of all because the
aristocracy of the press corps and the governmental elite
were such good friends. Joseph Alsop in his memoirs re-
called the nuances of the game as it used to be played
with the abandon of an *ancien regime* grandee:

"It is a myth that many government secrets are leaked at Washington dinner parties. Having people in power at your table is important and useful for two basic reasons. In the first place, one might get a line on the character of a person in power by seeing him or her informally at a dinner table. Second, especially if he or she sees you at your own dinner table, the official may get a line on what kind of person you may be and can decide, on the basis of this, whether you are trustworthy. This, in turn, lays a foundation for the right business relationship between the reporter and the man in power. . . ." (*I've Seen the Best of It*, Norton, 1992, pp. 388–389.)

Alsop describes a most genteel and socially ordered way of getting "a line on the character of a person in power." The birth of the character issue in our time—the proposition that we need to know (and nothing genteel about it) what stuff our leaders are made of in order to choose them well—is generally agreed to be at Watergate. And many of the roots of Watergate—the break-in to the office of Daniel Ellsberg's psychiatrist, President Nixon's efforts to inhibit critics and silence dissent, the tendency to unchecked presidential fiat, the Nixon presidency in the first place—are in Vietnam. In the wake of two unprecedented experiences of national tragedy and disgrace, each of which ruined a presidency, a profound distrust of our leaders took hold. In this the press, as recently as the Kennedy administration content with a posture of worshipfulness toward the White House, acted as the people's surrogate. We of the press invoked the cautionary wisdom of old, "Fool me once, shame on you; fool me twice, shame on me."

One commentator on the rise of the character issue, Larry J. Sabato, observes that the old code that shielded powerful politicians from scrutiny gave much more cover to Lyndon Johnson's and Richard Nixon's private lives than they could hope for today, even as their administrations and public persona turned to ashes. Nevertheless, as Michael Schudson writes in his new book, *Watergate in American Memory*, the tapes of Richard Nixon's private conversations with his advisors had a devastating effect on his public standing: "The president's talk was foul, vengeful, full of ethnic slurs; it was particularly shocking to morally upright Republicans." (*Watergate in American Memory: How We Remember, Forget and Reconsider the Past*, Basic Books, 1992, p. 20.)

Nixon destroyed himself to a great extent with his own words, for as the transcripts of the tapes were broadcast and reprinted night after night, they entangled him deeper and deeper in his own scheming. The other element of language-as-dynamite in Watergate was the relentless news reporting of Bob Woodward and Carl Bernstein of *The Washington Post*. The pen went up against the sword, and the pen prevailed. The fine movie based on Woodward and Bernstein's book, *All the Presidents' Men*, opens and closes with the sound and image of the reporters' words hammering out in teletype, ultimately drowning out the cannon fire at Nixon's second inaugural. Those who controlled the words now had the power and, it seemed, the duty to probe and question as deeply as they could those who aspired to control our national destiny.

In 1974 came Watergate's climax and coda: After the resignation and the succession came the pardon, by President Ford, of Nixon. It was inevitable that the 1976 campaign would focus on morality and character. "I'll never lie to you," said Jimmy Carter—a salute to the morality of language.

The press's and the public's discovery that President Carter and *his* men had warts was a letdown all the more because an ideal of moral purity had ridden so high. And there was another twist on the character issue. Compounding Carter's problems in wrestling with intractable issues of inflation, gas prices, and the hostage crisis was the extent to which he had staked his presidency on his piety, which now translated as ineffectuality.

For the press, however, the result was not a new sense of balance about the character issue, but rather, a deepening of the presumption of suspicion and mistrust. Schudson recalls the spirit of the times, quoting Ben Bradlee of *The Washington Post*: Young reporters were covering "the most routine rural fires as if they were Watergate and would come back and argue that there was gasoline in the hose and the fire chief was an anti-Semite and they really thought that was the way to fame and glory." (*Id.*, p. 119.) Bob Woodward explained his attitude about a peccadillo involving the Carter White House this way: "You have to remember that our experience for the past ten or fifteen years has been that in the end the government official always ended up being guilty as charged." (*Id.*, p. 129.)

The anti-establishmentarianism of the 1960s and Watergate begat the "opening" of the national political campaign process. Primaries and caucuses replaced smoke-filled rooms from sea to shining sea. But as we now know, the real result was an endless campaign and the need for candidates to project themselves in a marathon sequence of media marketing displays. And the real result of that was the triumph of the media consultants and their stratagems for selling positive images for their clients and destroying those of opposing candidates.

Much has been written in recent years about our TV-dominated culture of hype, long on entertainment and personalities, short on attention span, a culture of escapism and soundbites. Cultural historians note the breakthrough events in television programming that have led to a blur between news and entertainment: the launching in 1968 of *60 Minutes*, the popularity of which converted the CBS news division from a loss leader to a profit center, and in 1971 of *All in the Family*, which brought social issues such as racism, homosexuality, and drugs into nonnews, prime-time formats.

These last two decades were also the years when scores of major, independent newspapers and the three major television networks were being absorbed into vast corporate conglomerates. One result of these several trends taken together, as First Amendment scholar Rodney Smolla notes, is that the legal system, and especially juries, have come to see what we call the free press as just another business. (*Suing the Press: Libel, the Media and Power*, Oxford University Press, 1986, p. 12.)

Another widely recognized consequence of these trends is that ever more profit-driven media are under intensified pressure to reach readers and viewers, who in turn are more difficult to attract and hold in the face of new media alternatives and other distractions. That means an emphasis on what titillates, and on triaging what is judged "BO-ring," as young people and newsroom editors put it. And that means that public officials' private lives and personal problems are more newsworthy (less "BO-ring") than are complicated issues of governance.

Neither disillusionment with the Vietnam War nor disgust with Watergate nor all the abundant analysis of the culture of hype seems to me adequate to explain the new obsession with public officials' private lives, however. The traumas of Vietnam and Watergate were profound, but much has happened to ease them back into history, including a popular war and a popular presidency, and there are new poll statistics to show that the younger generation is growing up ignorant of Watergate in particular. The worst media offenders, TV shows like *Hard Copy* and *A Current Affair*, are not creative cultural forces driving the obsession, but derivative ones.

The more compelling reason why the idea of public service has become something of a joke and why public officials and candidates for office are cannon fodder for journalistic character inspection is that *government doesn't work*. If government doesn't work, then what people in its top ranks and aspiring to be there do is, essentially, act out roles. The more the job description has to do with image, and the less it has to do with substance, the more the press is of a mind to treat officeholders and candidates as "personalities." And the less it is inclined to rate their work according to any scale but that of how well they manage their personalities.

When government did work, the bond of trust that existed between press and the peers of officialdom was real. By the same token, a powerful and effective leader might be known all over town as a rogue, but if his effectiveness yielded notable results, those counted for more than his roguishness. Lyndon Johnson in the pre-Vietnam phases of his career is an example.

More than a few pre-Woodward-and-Bernstein journalists were clear-eyed, tough, and independent, though they dined with the mighty. With millions of their readers, listeners, and viewers, they felt genuine respect for those from the office of president on down who confronted the Depression, waged and won World War II, rebuilt the post-war world, and put government to work to further racial and economic justice at home. But the respect and sometimes reverence of the generation of James Reston, Walter Lippmann, and Edward R. Murrow for the generation of Franklin Delano Roosevelt, George Marshall, and Dean Acheson, and respect if not reverence for the generation that believed with Lyndon Johnson that government could build a Great Society, is gone. The root cause of this change is that the evidence is so overwhelming that the government of this country is not the effective instrument it once was. On the contrary, the problems of the nation seem to defeat efforts to combat them. The candidate for high office who claims to have a plan to solve them is regarded as a charlatan or an egomaniac.

The Restons and Murrows covered not only heroic figures but charlatans and egomaniacs, like Joe McCarthy, and they had the ability to discern and expose them. Today's journalists covering politics and what passes for government operate in an environment in which there are few if any towering, heroic figures to cover, few Marshall Plan or Great Society enterprises to cover, and that much more charlatanism and playacting to expose. Those who do the covering, therefore, look, and sometimes feel, that much more towering themselves.

Of his role as what came to be called a character cop in the 1988 presidential campaign, Paul Taylor of *The Washington Post* wrote:

> "We are reporters in an age when personality and image dominate politics the way party and ideology once did. This shift has had everything to do with the ubiquity and intrusiveness of modern

communications technology. It is beside the point to argue whether the change has been for the better. One cannot uninvent television . . . . Nor can one wish away the simple truth that as our culture has become more media-soaked, the way we conduct political campaigns and measure political leaders has become more personality-soaked."

No regrets there. "Indeed," writes Taylor,

"somebody had to prune the field, 'to get rid of the funny ones,' as one 1988 campaign manager put it. It simply wasn't practical for the voters to make choices among a dozen or more contenders." (*See How They Run: Electing a President in an Age of Mediocracy*, Knopf, 1990, pp. 10, 15.)

On the night of Saturday, May 2, 1987, four reporters and a photographer from *The Miami Herald*, acting on a tip that Gary Hart was due for an assignation with a young woman, staked out his home in Washington, D.C. On the basis of the stakeout, which all accounts now agree was incomplete, the *Herald* ran a story the next day across the top of its front page that began, "Gary Hart, the Democratic presidential candidate who has dismissed allegations of womanizing, spent Friday night and most of Saturday in his Capitol Hill town house with a young woman who flew from Miami and met him. Hart denied any impropriety. . . ." The same day, *The New York Times Sunday Magazine* ran a profile of Hart that quoted him saying of the media's interest in his private life, "Follow me around. I don't care. I'm serious. If anybody wants to put a tail on me, go ahead. They'd be very bored." (Jack W. Germond and Jules Witcover, *Whose Broad Stripes and Bright Stars:*

The Trivial Pursuit of the Presidency, Warner Books, 1989, pp. 182, 191.)

The woman's name, Donna Rice, and the fact that she had earlier traveled to Bimini with Hart on a boat called the *Monkey Business* quickly became the stuff of infamy. In his book *What It Takes: The Way to the White House*, Richard Ben Cramer, who won a Pulitzer Prize as a reporter for *The Philadelphia Inquirer*, evokes gonzo-fashion the madness that ensued:

> "That sent the pack over the edge. It was feral. It was without thought. Hart was catching the dread and fatal affliction—he was ridiculous. Even callow wannabe-big-feet could smell blood on the forest floor. Someone was gonna . . . *take Hart down.* . . . There was ineluctable logic to the chase: Hart was on the run. They had to show him embattled, fighting the iron ring, or dodging the cameras. That just meant more cameras, more bodies straining in the scum, more fights, more noise, more video-rodeo to get the tape of Hart fleeing . . . which, of course, only made him more furtive, the hunted beast. . . . " (Random House, 1992, p. 461.)

Meanwhile, *The Washington Post* had information, including a private detective's report, that Hart was involved with another woman as recently as the previous December. Next stop, a press conference in Hanover, New Hampshire, three days after the *Herald* story ran. Cramer's version:

> "The room should have held eighty to a hundred, but the pack was two-hundred strong . . . and, of course, there were tripods, cables, long lenses

banging shoulders and skulls of the newsmen
nearby, boom mikes poking crazily toward the
front of the room, lights ablaze on spindly poles or
burning hot white on the shoulders of the camera-
men. It had to be a hundred degrees . . . . People in
smelly suits, sweating, waiting . . . like a New York
summer subway, stuck in the tunnel . . . . *C'MON.
Whatsa HOLDUP?*" (*Id.*, p. 474.)

Post reporter Paul Taylor put to Hart the scarlet question, "Have you ever committed adultery?" Conversations between Taylor and Hart's high command, which
subsequently included *Post* editor Ben Bradlee, then
conveyed the implicit message that if Hart withdrew
from the race, the *Post* would not run its story. Hart left
the race two days later. (*See How They Run*, p. 66.)

What is remembered about the resolution of the Hart
case is the stance of *The Miami Herald* and *The Washington Post* as hanging judges. Suzanne Garment wrote
in *The Wall Street Journal* in 1992, "Journalists had
taken the front-runner for a major party's presidential
nomination and made him history in a breathtakingly
swift and direct way, without the need of intervention by
voters or other politicians." ("How Bill Clinton Got Away
With It," *Wall Street Journal*, March 2, 1992.) Less
publicized were the problems a number of men and
women of the press had with the episode. Three of *The
New York Times'* columnists, across the ideological spec-
trum, Anthony Lewis, A.M. Rosenthal, and William
Safire, expressed disgust. Lewis: "When I read about
The Miami Herald story on Gary Hart, I felt degraded in
my profession." Rosenthal: "I did not become a news-
paperman to hide outside a politician's house to find out
whether he was in bed with somebody." Safire wrote that

had he been asked the adultery question, he would have replied, "Go to hell." (*Whose Broad Stripes*, pp. 212–213.)

They are columnists and editors. But Taylor's own colleague on the reporting staff of the *Post*, the late Bill Peterson, refused to join him in working on the story of Hart's romantic involvements. Taylor writes in his account of the experience:

> "He thought the hour was late, the tip was weak and the story was sleazy. He worried that we were setting a precedent that would take us into the bedrooms of every other presidential candidate. I said this was a special case; the circumstances left us no choice; etc. But as I heard myself yammering, I realized—and it came as a shock—that there was more than one perspective on all this, even within my own shop." (*See How They Run*, p. 54.)

There are lingering ironies from the Hart case. Some of *The Washington Post*'s insight into the candidate's life-style derived from the fact that Hart had, during one of his separations from his wife, Lee, briefly rented an apartment in the house of Bob Woodward of Watergate fame. Ben Bradlee, nemesis of a powerful President, and now the force Hart had to answer to or yield to, personifies the post-Watergate power of the press. Finally, the late returns on the whole affair from reporters on the 1988 campaign who wrote books about it demonstrated not only that there were big holes in *The Miami Herald*'s stakeout but that Donna Rice probably did not spend the night at Hart's house and possibly never went to bed with him at all. Hanged for a lamb.

In the wake of the Gary Hart case came a wave of quick ends to the public careers of two other powerful men, their private lives laid out in the press: Speaker Jim

Wright of the House of Representatives and Secretary of Defense-designate John Tower. Wright's successor, Speaker Thomas Foley, survived a rumor-driven assault on his private character, but the overall climate was one that invited metaphors of the hunt, the kill, and the meal. "I'm very concerned about what's happening to government," Senator John Danforth of Missouri had said about an earlier episode, involving Jimmy Carter's budget director, Bert Lance: "I think we're eating ourselves alive." (*Watergate in American Memory*, p. 163.)

The atmosphere was the more poisonous because, after the Hart scandal, news organizations were less certain than ever about how to deal with tips, leaks, and salacious stories. Political operatives knew this. Shortly after the political demise of Wright and Tower, *The New York Times* reported that many journalists "are concerned about the degree to which they are manipulated by politicians on the attack, and they worry that the pressure resulting from competition among news organizations can lead to a lowering of standards of inquiry." (June 7, 1989, p. A25.)

Two powerful politicians inflicted personal disasters on themselves two decades ago—Edward Kennedy at Chappaquiddick, Wilbur Mills at the Tidal Basin—that stand out as landmarks of how "the system" used to work. Both were known by the Washington press corps to be prone to personal excesses; both were protected by that press corps until the scandals they perpetrated made protection impossible.

Those who followed them into the annals of political scandal are not so clearly or simply categorized as cases of the self-wounded. Press probe and revelation, and/or leaks of information or rumor to the press, are an aspect of their experiences. A list of political figures whose private lives or character has been the subject of deserved or dubious, brief or extended controversy over the last twenty years now include, along with Senators Hart and Tower and Congressmen Wright and Foley, Senator Thomas Eagleton; Congresswoman Geraldine Ferraro; Congressman Jack Kemp; Senator Joseph Biden; the Reverend Pat Robertson; Governor Richard Celeste; Mayor Henry Cisneros; Supreme Court nominees Robert Bork, Douglas Ginsburg, and Clarence Thomas; Congressman Tony Coelho; Congressman Barney Frank; Senator Charles Robb; Senator Brock Adams; and, in 1988, Michael Dukakis, Dan Quayle, and George Bush. The Hart case was only the most sensational and dramatically developed, featuring as it did both the politician *and* the adversarial press in roles worthy of Shakespeare.

From "Charisma" to "Character Issue"

Shocking posthumous revelations about the personal lives of two revered leaders, Franklin D. Roosevelt and John F. Kennedy, flowed into this shift in cultural and political attitude. They formed a historical backdrop to the self-questioning and acrimony among journalists about rules and boundaries of press coverage in contemporary cases like Hart's.

Hart himself was arguably the ablest and most thoughtful potential candidate of his party for the 1988 presidential nomination in matters of public policy, and the strong front-runner. He was a self-styled "Kennedyesque" politician, and successful because of it. His own rejection of news media demands and anger at their presumption and methods, which he articulated to the annual convention of newspaper publishers in the midst of the controversy, marks his 1987 career crisis as a turning point in the evolution of both the privacy issue and the balance of power between press and politician.

In 1971, two years after Chappaquiddick, a year before Watergate, Joseph P. Lash published *Eleanor and Franklin* and brought the most godlike figure of the American Century closer to earth. The myth had held that polio transformed FDR's character and the Roosevelts' marriage. There had been previous allegations of FDR's extramarital involvements. But now we knew on an authoritative basis (and one friendly to the Roosevelts) that Eleanor's discovery of Franklin's affair with her secretary, Lucy Mercer, destroyed the marriage in all but facade and was a crucial factor, along with the polio, in the transformation of both Roosevelts—hitherto somewhat inconsequential characters in the eyes of such well-informed contemporaries as Walter Lippmann and Alice Longworth—into formidable public figures.

Lash's book forced a re-estimation of Roosevelt the man, though for some it only underscored the extent to which a political leader should be measured on his public record, for the revelation did not detract from FDR's accomplishments as president. Indeed, it and subsequent disclosures about his selfishness and coldness toward others argued for the theory that a truly great national leader must be capable of freeing him or herself from personal constraints and obligations. ("I was one of those who served his purposes," Eleanor Roosevelt had written with edged stoicism after FDR's death.) No one yet could claim to have captured the whole FDR in biographical portraiture, but we had been forced to a more sophisticated, less sentimental sense of him. Meanwhile, Lash's book helped raise questions about the veils contemporary powerful politicians wear in their lifetimes and about the role of the press in conspiracies of silence, benign or otherwise.

Revelations about John F. Kennedy's steamy personal life, the most explosive of which were by-products of post-Watergate congressional investigations of the CIA and the FBI in the mid-1970s, were shocking in their details, but not, to some political insiders and members of the press corps, in theme. What the press had to contend with now, in the 1970s and 1980s, was the question whether it had been complicit in Kennedy's double life.

Kennedy had, after all, pulled off an elaborate wink. His "charisma," as the press called it, came in several parts, and one of them was a reputation for breaking all manner of taboos, an aura of sexual excitement. Norman Mailer's celebration of Kennedy's cool, hip, suavely ruthless style in a memorable 1960 *Esquire* essay, "Superman Comes to the Supermarket" (and in a fictional treatment of such a politician, part JFK, part Mailer, in his 1965 novel *An American Dream*), not only helped set Kennedy apart from the dull, reliable presidential style of the Eisenhower years. Such treatment also helped set the tone for a time—the famously swinging 1960s—when a buzz about a powerful politician or candidate's extramarital liaisons became standard equipment, a certification of a politician's "charisma," not so different from the glamorous auras of rock stars and their groupies. That Richard Nixon was an exception to this rule was evidence back then, for journalists and insiders, that he was (as was later said of Gary Hart) introverted and weird.

In the quarter-century since Kennedyesque politicians had an advantage over "square" ones like Eisenhower or Nixon, an era of optimism and hedonism turned to one of war, assassination, epic inflation, and end of empire. Women entered journalism and public life in force and broke up the old men's club rules governing press coverage of politics. And two highly astute politicians, Lyndon Johnson and Richard Nixon, stumbled so badly as to give politics a bad name, with Watergate all but institutionalizing that bad name.

If Mailer's "literary" treatment of Kennedy as an amoral, early postmodern hip hero set the tone for the 1960s, the young historian Michael Beschloss's *The Crisis Years: Kennedy and Khrushchev, 1960–1963* sets the tone for the 1990s. Beschloss weaves the troubling, often astonishingly brazen record of Kennedy's private behavior as President into the fabric of diplomatic history so as to leap past the filtered, compartmentalized treatments of the man by his hagiographers on the one hand and single-minded detractors on the other. Beschloss shows how closely interwoven the two sides of Kennedy's life were; how obsessive and intrusive into the presidential schedule his sexual liaisons were; and how, regarding current liaisons, Kennedy was vulnerable to blackmail by foreign governments, the Mafia, and the director of the FBI. Additionally, Kennedy's amphetamine-based treatments by a cafe society "Dr. Feelgood" may have affected his diplomacy. Beschloss's presentation of the case of Kennedy is one in which the pieces of the life do not separate out, public and private. They need to be weighed together if one is to reach a balanced evaluation of his presidency. (Harper-Collins, 1991, pp. 187–189, 610–617.)

"They can't touch me while I'm alive," Kennedy is supposed to have said of his scandalous behavior, "and after I'm dead, who cares?" What is the difference between the attempt by a scrupulous, thoughtful historian like Beschloss to answer that question and the journalistic character issue gauntlet a politician or candidate for high office must run today?

One way of addressing the issue is this: What we might loosely call "the Watergate era" forced up the standard for evaluating those who ask for the public's trust. In attempting to perform its duty, holding public officials to account according to higher standards, the press bites off more than it can chew. While history and biography deal with vast archives of record, there are limits to journalism's methods. Journalism cannot claim to have the last word; in the late Philip Graham's famous formulation, it is the first draft of history. Journalism's claims are meant to be fact-based, verifiable, sourced (all too often, of necessity if journalism is to probe, anonymously sourced) efforts to record events as they happen and states of play as they evolve. But weighed against their often breathtaking force is the extent to which those efforts can and will be supplemented, or perhaps upended, tomorrow or the next day.

Although historical and biographical evaluations are intrinsically retrospective, character issue journalism operates on a highly charged field of action. It influences voters who, in the absence of strong parties or compelling debate on issues, are searching for criteria to help them decide how to cast their ballots. It has the potential to transform public officials' lives dramatically and disastrously while they live.

Political figures may do themselves in and blame their problems on the press, in which case the question of the destructive power of the media is ambiguous. The First Amendment means, in part, that the press in this country has the right to scrutinize those who would govern us, and from this and other basic tenets of democracy flow the press's duty to do so. But a vagueness in standards for evaluation of public officials today, together with the enormity of the mega-media effect when unleashed, yields a spectacle akin to a hurricane or wildfire driving animals mad.

This anarchic state of affairs is reflectéd in the publication of two recent books attempting to make sense of it. *Feeding Frenzy: How Attack Journalism Has Transformed American Politics* (The Free Press, 1991) by Larry J. Sabato, professor of government at the University of Virginia, focuses on press coverage of political figures. *Scandal: The Culture of Mistrust in American Politics* (Random House, 1991) by Suzanne Garment, resident scholar at the American Enterprise Institute and former columnist for *The Wall Street Journal*, concerns itself with issues of ethics in politics and government. Both are highly critical of contemporary journalistic practices and skeptical of the usual media rationales for those practices.

Neither writer is naive enough to think that we have suffered a journalistic fall from an age of grace. Sabato cites de Tocqueville's expression of distaste in 1835 for American journalists' "vulgar turn of mind" and their tendency to "assail the characters of individuals, to track them into private life and disclose all their weaknesses and vices." Garment notes that scandals, especially sex scandals, are as old as those that bedeviled founding fathers Hamilton and Jefferson.

Nevertheless, Sabato sees an erosion in journalism's standards today, with dire results, for if the press does not honor its First Amendment protection with a concern for fairness and responsibility, he argues, it makes a mockery of political discourse, encourages cynicism about public life, and ultimately damages its own credibility as a check on government.

Sabato is careful to say that the feeding frenzy syndrome is not as absent of rationale as it seems when it takes the field. He writes with sophistication about the fact that since Vietnam and Watergate, journalists are more determined to get at the truth behind the official version of truth than was an earlier generation. (He does not cite the memorable line of *The New York Times'* Russell Baker that he left daily reporting for his op-ed column because he was tired of being lied to by politicians.) To what seem like mindless feeding frenzies there is usually, as Sabato puts it, a "subtext," a layer of thesis or suspicion about the more subtle aspects of the public official in question that is, thanks to the immediate controversy, suddenly apparent to be reported upon. The Gary Hart-Donna Rice relationship surfaced a subtext that Hart was at once aloof and reckless—somewhat "weird" in his attitude that his fine and original mind justified a conceit that nothing could touch him. The subtext of the Dukakis "mental health" story was that the Governor's image as a flawlessly equipped technocrat could not be the whole story. These subtexts strengthen journalists' resolve that they are in pursuit of something more significant than a gaffe or a wart. (*Feeding Frenzy*, pp. 72–73, 76.)

But what if they are pursuing spiced red herring or pure gossip fed out by partisan operatives gunning for political enemies? The traffic in damaging personal detail that helped deny Senate confirmation to John Tower as President Bush's Secretary of Defense triggered revenge in the form of damaging leaks about Democratic House leaders Wright, Coelho, and Foley. The technique is hardly new; it dominated Washington in Andrew Jackson's administration. What is striking about it today is that the press is at such a loss about how to deal with it.

Sabato is a political scientist, Suzanne Garment somewhat more a partisan. (Her husband, Leonard Garment, was President Nixon's White House counsel and, as she notes, has represented Reagan administration appointees caught up in legal controversy.) Vietnam and Watergate bred a "self-reinforcing scandal machine," she writes. Prosecutors, legislative staffers, executive branch investigators, and journalists use each other today to advance their immediate professional interests in unprecedented numbers and media impact. Since Watergate, Garment argues, there is an absolutism, a nihilism, a blend of "prudery and prurience" that has taken legitimate reform measures to the extreme. Her sometimes-arch rhetoric draws on the neoconservative canon: "[T]oday's ethics police practice scorched-earth warfare of a sort readily recognizable from Vietnam days." The resultant mindset of "scandal politics," Garment contends, is that we demand a "politics of virtue" so pure and free of the realities of compromise and interest group trading as to be innocent of reality. We need now, she concludes, to relegate "political scandal back to its perennial, venerated, and distinctly secondary place in American public life." (*Scandal*, pp. 9, 38, 184, 287–288, 303–304.)

These books have helped fortify a sense in the land that the press does indeed have a problem. But they go only so far—not much beyond the Beltway—in comprehending that problem. For its part, the press scratches itself about the problem (indeed, it regularly quotes writers like Sabato as authorities in articles about privacy and scandal.) But the press also tends to deny this problem. Above all, it does not know what to do about it.

The press says, as a matter of professional identity, and I myself have said as a journalist, that our business is facts, the public has a right to know them, freedom has a price, we let the chips fall where they may, we are not in the philosophy business. It says, if we adopt common-sense rules in these matters as written internal codes, not only will they fail to cover the next sensitive case, but we will transgress them slightly, or innocently, and thereby give libel plaintiffs yet another weapon against us with which to erode the First Amendment on spurious or technical grounds. It says, no one got into this business to be loved; weighty reflection about our role is for journalism schools and op-ed pages, not for the reporter and the editor under the gun or on the trail of the next Watergate.

But influential press figures also say, as former *Atlanta Constitution* editor and Nieman Foundation curator Bill Kovach remarked of the publication of rumors in cases like that of House Speaker Thomas Foley, "We didn't used to do that." And many journalists agree with Abe Rosenthal, former executive editor of *The New York Times*, writing in the wake of the Hart affair:

> "We are begging the nation to treat us as unworthy of respect. In time, without any question, we will lose the support of the American people in our constant struggles against those who would erode the First Amendment. We cannot claim it was designed for voyeurs." (*Feeding Frenzy*, pp. 199, 204.)

To Be Let Alone

The process by which our culture became more open and frank, a process that included the disclosure of secrets like Roosevelt's, Kennedy's, and Hart's, paralleled a legal evolution that greatly strengthened press protection under the First Amendment (or, if you prefer, liberalized the law). Both evolutions have, however, left anything but settled boundaries between those in the business of reporting and commenting, and those being reported and commented upon.

At one level, all is clear: Under the 1964 *Times v. Sullivan* decision and subsequent Supreme Court decisions in libel and privacy cases, speech about all aspects of public figures is protected under the First Amendment, provided it is not published with knowing or reckless disregard of its falsity. Justice William Brennan wrote for the Court in *Sullivan*: "[W]e consider this case against the background of a profound national commitment to the principle that debate on public issues should be uninhibited, robust, and wide-open, and that it may well include vehement, caustic, and sometimes unpleasantly sharp attacks on government and public officials." (Quoted in Anthony Lewis, *Make No Law: The Sullivan Case and the First Amendment*, Random House, 1991, p. 143.)

Lewis reminds us that Justice Brennan wrote the decision

> "in the grand style, reordering a whole area of the law as few modern Supreme Court opinions do—or can, really. . . . Justice Brennan's opinion took the libertarian arguments of Brandeis, Holmes and others and wove the threads into the first full statement by the Supreme Court as a whole of an American theory of free speech: the Madisonian theory. The opinion adopted Madison's view that the citizens are sovereign in the United States, and that their freedom to criticize the government is 'the central meaning of the First Amendment.' It treated free speech as not just an individual right but a political necessity." (*Id.*, pp. 153, 155.)

One of the most significant ways the *Sullivan* decision emboldened the press was that it articulated First Amendment protection for criticism of public officials even when a news organization got some of the facts wrong, as was the case with the civil rights leaders' advertisement in *The New York Times* that triggered the *Sullivan* suit. Lewis writes, "The allowance of room for honest mistakes of fact encouraged the press, in particular, to challenge official truth on two subjects so hidden by government secrecy, Vietnam and Watergate, that no unauthorized story could ever have been 'absolutely confirmable.'" (*Id.*, p. 158.)

In decision after decision since *Sullivan*, the Court has also afforded the press protection under the First Amendment when it deals in information concerning *private* figures, when that information is deemed of public concern or newsworthy, and—even if it is found to be false—when the news organization cannot be found negligent in publishing it.

The Court has of course also shown qualified concern for those whom the news media cover. Since 1890, when Louis Brandeis, then in private practice, and his law partner Samuel Warren argued for the right "to be let alone" by a press "that is overstepping in every direction the obvious bounds of propriety and decency," a law of privacy has slowly evolved. (Quoted in Richard F. Hixson, *Privacy in a Public Society*, Oxford University Press, 1987, pp. 31–32.) "Gossip," wrote Brandeis and Warren, "is no longer the resource of the idle and of the vicious, but has become a trade, which is pursued with industry as well as effrontery. To satisfy a prurient taste the details of sexual relations are spread broadcast in the columns of the daily papers. To occupy the indolent, column upon column is filled with idle gossip, which can

only be procured by intrusion upon the intimate circle."
(Katherine M. Galvin and Stephen Elias, *Media Law: A Legal Handbook for the Working Journalist*, Nolo Press, 1984, pp. 197–198.) They of course were lawyers, and as Hixson notes, their view was that of an upper class offended by the new popular press. Interestingly, Hixson cites an article in *Scribner's Magazine* the same year by the influential journalist of the day E.L. Godkin, arguing that privacy was threatened by undue curiosity about other people's business: In all this," he argued, "the advent of the newspaper, or rather of a particular class of newspaper, had made a great change. It has converted curiosity into what economists call an effectual demand, and gossip into a marketable commodity." (*Privacy in a Public Society*, p. 29.) In contrast to the sorting out of the constitutional standards governing libel law since *Sullivan*, the standard for invasion of privacy is unclear and evolving. Hixson compares the Supreme Court in its First Amendment decisions since *Sullivan* to a juggler, with the interests of reputation, privacy, and the media as three balls in the air. With respect to the first of these, Justice Potter Stewart has written that "the right of a man to the protection of his reputation from unjustified invasion and wrongful hurt reflects no more than our basic concept of the essential dignity and worth of every human being." (*Id.*, p. 177.) In *Gertz v. Welch* (1974), the Court leaned back from protecting speech and found that a private person has protection from false and recklessly published statements, regardless of whether the information is a matter of public concern or not. (Quoted in *Make No Law*, p. 192.)

In *Herbert v. Lando* (1979), the Court set another significant rule for the press. Here it held for libel plaintiffs' right to examine—to "discover"—reporters' notes and other internal documents. The logic flowed from the Court's exception of protection for the press in *Sullivan*, when publication was made with knowing or reckless falsity. As Anthony Lewis explains, "[I]f a person criticized on the air or in print believes that the writer or broadcaster was aware of the truth and omitted it, how can he find out without exploring the editorial process?" (*Id.*, p. 201.)

The *Herbert* decision in turn helped embolden two distinctly public figures, Generals William Westmoreland and Ariel Sharon, each to sue powerful news organizations for libel in the winter of 1984—Westmoreland sued CBS and Sharon sued *Time* magazine. Both suits were concerned with damage to reputation rather than invasion of privacy, but each aimed at what it depicted as an arrogant, imperial, malicious news media in ways that connected with the privacy concern. Although neither Westmoreland nor Sharon recovered damages, each embarrassed his press tormentor in the process by demonstrating shoddy and unprofessional journalistic practice. The libel suit of Mobil Chief Executive Officer William Tavoulareas against *The Washington Post* for a story alleging that he had set his son up in business similarly embarrassed that newspaper in the 1980s. The discovery process brought out the stated desire of Bob Woodward, by now a key *Post* editor, for what he called "holy shit" stories—reporting that would stop readers in their tracks—and this helped Tavoulareas win two rounds of court decisions, in 1983 and 1985, until the *Post* finally prevailed in the U.S. Court of Appeals in 1987.

Rodney Smolla writes that by the time of the *Sharon* case in particular, in which the judge had especially harsh words for *Time*'s arrogance in the discovery process (as did the jury for *Time*'s negligence), "one sees the emergence of a social issue that is quite clearly coming to the forefront of the American consciousness: that the public's 'right to know' *includes the right to know how critical media decisions are made.*" (*Suing the Press*, pp. 94–95, author's emphasis.)

Meanwhile, a related trend in libel litigation began to dog the press: the tendency of juries in lower courts to award huge damages to libel plaintiffs (some of them public figures, such as the actress Carol Burnett, successfully claiming intrusion upon their privacy as well as defamation). Even when these cases are overturned on appeal or sharply reduced, and almost all are, the cost of pursuing them is often impossible for any but major news organizations able to afford libel insurance and court costs. These suits, often handled by lawyers working on contingency fees, thus permit plaintiffs to "win by suing," as one commentator puts it, even if they cannot "sue to win." (Professor Randall Bezanson, quoted in Floyd Abrams, "Why We Should Change Libel Law," *The New York Times Sunday Magazine*, September 29, 1985, p. 87.)

Some scholars and critics have noted that forces deeper than psychic kick or revenge in the matter at hand are at work in the bringing of many of these suits against the media and in the juries' awards of enormous damages. For example, Smolla argues that as the agencies of government and the banking, retail, and corporate worlds built the details of common citizens' lives, including traffic records, credit ratings, and life-style preferences into vast, faceless, computerized data bases, they provoked a broad, anti-institutional reaction that parallels and blends with animus against the press. He writes, "The media's power to expose secrets, playing havoc with self-image and public image, is yet another erosion of the sanctity of individual human dignity, and the sympathy of American juries toward libel and invasion of privacy plaintiffs is a sort of grass-roots response to that erosion." (*Suing the Press*, p. 16.) It is a response, Anthony Lewis agrees, addressed to news organizations perceived as arrogant and unaccountable. He writes, "The networks, big newspapers and magazines ask questions and demand answers, but when anyone wants to know about their business, they wrap themselves in the First Amendment and refuse to answer." (*Make No Law*, p. 207.)

As can be seen, then, it is not only demagogues working the right wing fringe of American politics who talk about the arrogance of the news media. The *Westmoreland* and *Sharon* cases prompted two books by distinguished journalists troubled by what the press makes of its legal protection. In *Reckless Disregard*, Renata Adler writes:

> "[W]itnesses with a claim to any sort of journalistic affiliation [in the *Westmoreland* and *Sharon* cases] considered themselves a class apart, by turns lofty, combative, sullen, lame, condescending, speciously pedantic, but, above all, socially and, as it were, Constitutionally arrogant . . . . 'Who *are* these people?' is a question that would occur almost constantly to anyone upon reading or hearing the style and substance of their testimony." (*Reckless Disregard: Westmoreland v. CBS et al., Sharon v. Time*, Knopf, 1986, p. 133.)

It has been said that much of the posture Adler derides is common to all legal proceedings. But as one who has in my own journalistic career been drawn into defending major libel suits and been present at depositions and jury trials growing out of them, I recognize, and can testify to, the state of mind she characterizes. The libel case becomes a form of war. The *Herbert* decision gives a powerful procedural weapon to the plaintiff. If there is malice in the room, we, the defendant, holding the line for the rest of the press, know it is not in our professional nature but on the other side, in the hate-filled eyes of powerful politicians and public figures who resent the very idea of independent news coverage. And so we fall into the combat mode along with our crack attorneys: "Kill or be killed!"

Richard Clurman, former chief of correspondents for Time-Life news service, troubled by a number of signs of the times, including the behavior in the *Sharon* case of his former employer, writes in *Beyond Malice: The Media's Years of Reckoning*, "Reputation in journalism is about being right, not about being within the law. The only sin in journalism worse than being wrong is an unwillingness to admit it. So far as the public was concerned, *Time* had committed both sins." And he quotes Abraham Sofaer, the judge in the *Sharon* case: "The media have given too much weight to the law in deciding what they can do instead of deciding what they should do. The media, not the courts and particularly not media lawyers, should set the standards for their own conduct." (Transaction Books, 1988, pp. 170, 171.)

Just so. But the guidelines are few. A widely used journalism education text notes that as the standard of newsworthiness tends to prevail over that of privacy in court cases, most questions in this area are not in the end legal but rather ethical: Thus, "The question for most journalists is not whether to invade privacy, but how much." (H. Eugene Goodwin, *Groping for Ethics in Journalism*, Iowa University Press, 1987, p. 237.) For the thoughtful journalist seeking to set a compass by the law, there is this fundamental paradox, as the California Supreme Court has put it: "The right to know and the right to have others not know are, simplistically considered, irreconcilable." (California Supreme Court quoted in *Privacy in a Public Society*, p. 184.) The conflict between these values is dramatically evident when journalists' and researchers' efforts to secure information through The Freedom of Information Act, enacted in 1966 and flowing from the "right to know," are in specific cases stalemated by the 1974 Privacy Law, designed to protect the individual's personal privacy in the face of government information data gathering and sharing.

Fear of Embarrassment, Sacredness of Self

The youngest, greenest cub reporter generally comes face to face with the tension between the value of newsworthiness and that of privacy, for she or he has the task of asking the stricken parent, child, wife, husband, or friend for details and pictures of the loved one who has been kidnapped, killed, indicted, or otherwise caught in the headlights of onrushing news.

On the one hand, accepting the news story as one of the inevitable effects of the catastrophe, the interviewee will want the reported details to be faithful to the facts, at least to the extent of not compounding the pain with inaccuracy or distortion. Also, people in such circumstances sometimes find the sharing of the details, the processing of the loss, cathartic and comforting. On the other hand, the interviewee resents the fact of the story at some level, as part of the catastrophe for which it stands. No doubt there is fault to be found with the tone it strikes, the judgments it implies, the boundaries it crosses, or the detail it bungles no matter how hard the reporter tried to get everything right.

At the same time, that green reporter must learn detachment and skepticism, especially when a story touches close to home, and if she or he is a slow learner, a grizzled editor will drill it in. "If your mother says she loves you," goes the old maxim of Chicago journalism, "check it out."

Good journalists assimilate these basic training lessons in ways that help them make balanced decisions about privacy later in their careers. Depending on how well we as journalists make those decisions, we affect overnight, with more or less unpleasant aftertaste, the lives of others. That aftertaste turns up in opinion polls, not always articulately stated, as part of the count against the press on the arrogance charge. It is an attitude that can spring from a personal experience of being in or near these collisions between private life and news, whatever one feels for a Bill Clinton or an Arthur Ashe.

I have spent my share of difficult hours with colleagues in and out of the newsroom deciding whether to reveal a famous politician's indiscretion, whether to identify a prominent citizen's death as a suicide, whether to name relatives caught up in a public figure's imbroglio. At *The Boston Globe* we had advance word of Senator Paul Tsongas' cancer and decision to quit the Senate, and the drama in the newsroom whether to go with the story before the Senator revealed it on his own timetable (which included talking it through with his family) threatened to upstage the public event. Several such questions I helped decide on the side of newsworthiness, a few despite serious doubts. I can call up just by thinking about them, and the conversations surrounding them, the mental and physical unease I felt then, six or eight or ten years ago.

As editor of *The Boston Globe*, I also became something of a public figure in that city and was the subject of a number of stories in other media. To say that some of them were constructed of gossip would be to overpraise them for structure. I know what it feels like to read a story that bungles details about me and my family, attributes to me motivations and views I never held and acts I never committed, and alleges startlingly unpleasant aspects of my nature—according to unnamed sources. I came to recognize the telltale structure of stories in which the "reporter" gives over the space to the agendas of sources as garrulous as they are anonymous.

All of that went with the territory, as I saw it. Boston has an intense love-hate relationship with its paper of record (maybe hate-love better indicates the emphasis), a relationship that figures strongly in J. Anthony Lukas's fine account of the integration of the Boston schools, *Common Ground*. With a magazine rather than a hard-news background, I was an unlikely figure to emerge as the paper's editor and therefore the focus of a lot of anxious, and not a little hostile, interest within our own newsroom, a situation that fed the atmosphere of gossipy speculation.

Whether I was influenced by that experience or not, my own starchy instincts about covering the personal lives of others are these: I am with the late Bill Peterson of *The Washington Post*, who refused to join his colleague Paul Taylor in hunting down the final piece of paydirt on Gary Hart. ("Paul, you don't have to do this," an agitated Peterson said to Taylor, in Richard Ben Cramer's account, p. 472.) I would have refused to authorize the stakeout on Hart's house; my argument would have been that if his behavior was as out of control as the tip to *The Miami Herald* suggested, a less dubious means of verifying it would soon be at hand. I do not believe in publishing rumors, however much around town they are. The situational ethics exercises in mainstream newsrooms may indeed be a relic of a more civilized media environment and era, but I support them. However, I fear that they take place in something of a vacuum and that what we need to make better sense of the professional dilemmas is a larger context.

The confusion, the flaw, the fault, is not just the news media's—it is ours as a society, as human beings. The confusion in the news media about the boundaries of privacy is really a reflection of human ambivalence about privacy and secrets.

What "people" in the abstract (that supposedly hard and measurable "Public Opinion" we toss around in the news media) feel about cases like Gary Hart's is, I think, akin to what most of us feel when mishap, misstep, or scandal occurs very close to home—in our own neighborhood or town or our professional circle.

Who has not experienced what plays out in such a community and measured it, if only in passing, against what goes on in one's own head—that is, a mixture of fascination, regret, shock, communal embarrassment, empathy, pity, good fortune not to be so afflicted, amusement, titillation, eagerness to hear all the details, shame about such smallness in oneself, wish that the whole affair would disappear and the clock be set back to before it began, anger at those who are gossiping insensitively—all of this at once and making no coherent sense? If our feelings for the person on the spot are strongly negative, pure pleasure and the thrill of revenge are of course added to the mix. But most of the other elements are there, too, particularly shame at getting such a kick out of the meanness of scandal or the misfortune of others, at taking part in the casting of stones.

Often, part of us feels for the victim—sympathy, empathy, identification—and we share to a degree the victim's embarrassment. In the case even of Nixon, as of the local high-school principal or the town selectman enveloped in an ugly scandal, the embarrassment of the leader is also the embarrassment of the community.

When a leader in a given situation is thrown off by uncontrollable circumstances, the terms on which we have accepted that leader's dominance collapse, writes the sociologist Erving Goffman. The leader "may feel ashamed while the others present may feel hostile," he writes, "and all the participants may come to feel ill at ease, nonplussed, out of countenance, embarrassed, experiencing the kind of anomy that is generated when the minute social system of face-to-face interaction breaks down." (*The Presentation of Self in Everyday Life*, Doubleday-Anchor Edition, 1959, p. 12.) In larger public situations, too, that shared embarrassment and the impulse to deal with it are a driving force, so the candidate or public official under fire schedules a no-holds-barred press conference to clear the air and show there is nothing to hide. Reporters compete to pin the target of the scrutiny down in some new discrepancy. As the politician's embarrassment deepens, so does our involvement with it.

I believe that public opinion, like each of us in our own lives, participating in what amounts to vicarious invasion of the privacy of others, is a creature of mixed impulses and reactions. We are both intimately involved and distanced, perhaps disgusted; we can adjust our spot between these extremes according to mood, circumstance, or the company we are in.

The poet William Empson writes of the seventh and

most complex form of poetic ambiguity that it occurs when a word has two meanings and the author reveals the conflict between these two meanings in his own mind. For example, "the notion of what you want involves the idea that you have not got it . . . it marks a center of conflict; the notion of what you want involves the notion that you must not take it." (*Seven Types of Ambiguity*, Meridian Books, 1955, p. 193.)

Sociologists, psychologists, poets, and philosophers are more comfortable reflecting on such aspects of the communications process than are journalists. Sissela Bok, who has written on lying and secrets, muses on whether journalists and other professionals view secrets as "guilty" and "threatening," connoting impropriety, or "awesome and worthy of respect." She writes:

> "[I]t is almost as if the effort to define *secrecy* reflected the conflicting desires that approaching many an actual *secret* arouses: the cautious concern to leave it carefully sealed, or on the contrary, the determination to open it up, cut it down to size, see only one of its aspects, hasten to solve its riddle." (*Secrets: On the Ethics of Concealment and Revelation*, Vintage Books, 1989, p. 14.)

That duality in the meaning of secrecy parallels the tension in First Amendment law between freedom of expression (that is, the right to probe and speak) and the right to privacy. The problem for the journalist in the current climate is that compounding the duality of secrets and the vagueness of privacy law is the absence of a coherent professional code or logical, let alone ethical, context for deciding such questions. Hide-and-seek is a universal child's amusement, Bok writes. For children, it's all a game, and poking around in our parents' bedroom drawers or playing "I Spy" is a part of growing up. To mature, she adds, is to come to terms with such games and unbridled curiosity and to develop *discretion*.

Discretion, maturity of judgment in matters involving privacy, is precisely what journalism is struggling with today. The missing element seems to be self-awareness. Take the dynamic of the feeding frenzy. The scenario is as old as drama or legend. The prince, or king, has embarrassed himself and embarrassed us, public and the press alike, and while we may or may not feel some sympathy for him, we want the embarrassment to end. Moreover, we cannot sustain this whirl of titillation, this orgy of gossip. It is too consuming, and we are coming to hate ourselves a little for indulging it. For both public and press, it is time to get back to the rhythm of business as usual, plans for the picnic, cultivation of those aspects of our nature we take pride in and want others to admire.

At such moments, the press is framing the communal embarrassment, mediating it so society can come to terms with it. More than that, it is resolving the conflict, for as the drama plays out, the press is in the role of exorcist. The prince or the king must die so that the embarrassment can end. And the news media, like the witch or the shaman of primitive societies, have the power and the function to keep pushing the plot line, based on what "sources" say, to the ritual's end. (For a thoughtful and provocative treatment of this thesis, see "On Communicative Practice: The 'Other Worlds' of Journalism and Shamanism" by Barbie Zelizer in *Southern Folklore*, Vol. 49 [1992], pp. 19–36.)

Seen this way, those contradictory poll findings on public condemnation of an intrusive press back-to-back with public approval of a watchdog press make sense. To deal with the embarrassment of a public figure perceived as unworthy, society needs an exorcist—and is unhappy that it has that need. Society depends on the press to perform the work of ritual cleansing—and fears and resents the press for its power to do 'so.

But that is not the role the press acknowledges. Lacking self-awareness, it also lacks discretion. It is like an adolescent who has prematurely achieved height and strength. It is an exorcist wielding power in the dark—making it up as we go along, as Anna Quindlen put it.

There is one further wrinkle to this pattern of journalistic power without self-knowledge. We speak often and sweepingly in journalism of "the right to know" when what we mean is the right to access of information. We say that public officials forfeit much, even all, of their right to privacy when they ask for our mandate to determine our fate. We may debate whether they retain any rights in the matter: What we miss is the question of our presumption to measure that public figure's private self, to decide that character issue. It is interesting, I think, how mysterious to this day the inner characters and private selves of two of our greatest presidents, Abraham Lincoln and Franklin Roosevelt, remain, for all the words written about them.

"Human beings," Bok writes,

> "can be subjected to every scrutiny, and reveal much about themselves; but they can never be entirely understood, simultaneously exposed from every perspective, completely transparent either to themselves or to other persons. They are not only unique but unfathomable. The experience of such uniqueness and depth underlies self-respect and what social scientists have called the sense of 'the sacredness of the self.'"

She adds, "[T]he death of an individual has been likened to the burning down of a great library or to a universe going extinct, as the inwardness and focus and connections of a life are lost, along with the sense of what William Blake called 'the holiness of minute particulars.'" (*Secrets*, p. 219.)

Breaking the Cycle

Of course, the journalistic code does not press reporters to presume to know the holiest of another individual's minute particulars, to pretend to the historian or biographer's role. On the contrary, it speaks in terms of macho minimalism and fatalism: We are not in the philosophy or sociology business. Let the chips fall where they may.

What could or should the code say? How could it better take account of the ambiguities of privacy and convey the value of discretion? A number of scholars, critics, and practitioners have offered reasonable guidelines for self-regulation. (*Beyond Malice*, p. 263; *Feeding Frenzy*, pp. 218–219; *Scandal*, p. 197.) Many news organizations have at least general rules for reporters and editors, though, as noted, there is a widespread fear that a detailed, written, in-house code of ethics is a potentially lethal weapon in the hands of a libel plaintiff who can claim you have departed from your own standards.

The unanimous view in the news business is that anything like the aborted National News Council of the 1970s and early 1980s, initially funded by the Twentieth Century Fund and intended to critique news media practices and evaluate complaints, is a nonstarter for obvious and demonstrated reasons: It goes against every independent instinct of the American press and can have no teeth without going up against the First Amendment.

The widespread consensus regarding libel litigation holds that reform is overdue because so much of such litigation is undertaken in a spirit of revenge by subjects of news coverage claiming damage to reputation or peace of mind. Many First Amendment experts agree that one of the most practical and doable reforms would be for the news media to practice consistent, careful, and fair-minded acknowledgment or retraction of error, and provision for response or equal time, for those claiming to have been damaged or misrepresented by news coverage. ("I went to the paper," says the Paul Newman character in the film *Absence of Malice*, after an unscrupulous prosecutor has leaked an inaccurate story about him to a susceptible reporter. He is asked, "What did they say?" and responds, "Ever try to talk to a paper?") News organizations would thereby effectively reduce the volume of litigation and ease their own unlovely reputation for arrogance.

Groping for Ethics in Journalism, a journalism education text, samples some rules adopted by news organizations, such as *The Philadelphia Inquirer*, *The San Jose Mercury News*, and *The St. Paul Pioneer Press and Dispatch*, that have written codes. Thus, the *Inquirer* instructs reporters that private citizens caught

> "in tragic situations [or] thrust unwittingly and unwillingly into a public situation [are] likely to be unfamiliar with news-gathering practices. Staff members should clearly identify themselves when approaching such inexperienced people and treat them with courtesy." (*Groping for Ethics in Journalism*, p. 262.)

Several news organizations' codes state specifically that they do *not* identify the victims of child molestation or rape. (The latter custom was for years an example of clear professional consensus on a privacy issue—until the editors of *The Des Moines Register*, in collaboration with a rape victim, carefully and thoughtfully targeted the ambiguity implicit in the rule. They asked, does not anonymity further stigmatize the victim?) *The Detroit News* offers its reporters some guidelines for covering disasters and tragedies. These include:

"Say you are sorry and mean it. . . .

"Do not ask dumb questions.

"Do not break and enter in search of pictures or a comment. . . .

"Try not to be part of the story." (*Id.*, pp. 261, 263.)

Richard Clurman argues quite rightly that

"self-imposed restrictions are hardly inconceivable. On extreme occasions in the past, the media have voluntarily given up rights the law allows for values they themselves recognize as more important. After the urban riots in many cities during the late '60s and early '70s, the media collaborated with local government to create standards of coverage that helped reduce inflammatory tensions." (*Beyond Malice*, p. 222.)

Leslie Gelb of *The New York Times* rejects the self-serving quotient in the proposition that it is elitist for journalists to hold back sensitive information about public figures, noting that they "routinely exercise such judgment and withhold unsubstantiated or irrelevant information." ("Journalistic Cannibals," *The New York Times*, January 27, 1992, p. A-11.)

With these and other particulars, a number of commentators, including members of the journalistic profession, argue and practice the view that a degree of press self-regulation in matters involving the privacy of subjects of news coverage is acceptable, appropriate, and no threat to the First Amendment. The rub will always be in the urgency of the case in hand, the ambiguities of the story, the ethics of that particular situation. Never, in the heat of competitive and deadline pressure, will there be agreement about where to draw the line of discretion. And always, perhaps most riddlesome of all, will be the question of how much the public wants such disclosures and how much it does not.

I feel that arguments for press self-regulation concerning privacy will not be persuasive until or unless a news organization stumbles into its own catastrophe in the area of privacy comparable to *The Washington Post*'s position after reporter Janet Cooke's Pulitzer Prize-winning series on "Jimmy's World" was found to have been a fabrication. Against the backdrop of the *Post* returning its tainted Pulitzer, many news organizations, concerned about how safe they were from such a debacle, reviewed their standard guidelines for reporters and editors, and that is when some adopted codes of ethics.

Such a compounding of press transgressions of standards of privacy and decency, crossing some new line (for example, triggering an emotional collapse or suicide on the part of a subject of news coverage) and bringing outrage and demands for reform down upon the journalistic profession, is hardly beyond the realm of possibility. For instance, Elizabeth Hill, who with her husband, James Hill, brought a landmark "false light" privacy case against Time, Inc. in the 1960s, suffered what in the course of the suit was called lasting emotional injury because of *Life* magazine's depiction of her and her family as models for the book and play *The Desperate*

Hours, about a family held hostage by violent criminals. In 1971, four and a half years after the Supreme Court decided in favor of Time, Inc., Mrs. Hill committed suicide. More recently, the Arthur Ashe disclosure gave another taste of what such a case might be like. A repetition of a Gary Hart-like episode in circumstances less compromising for the politician and even more dubious for the news media is more than possible. The Clinton-Flowers episode suggested the new electronic angles that can come into play.

Meanwhile, experts on privacy law see a possibility that the Supreme Court might push back against the press on what is called the second of the four recognized privacy torts, disclosure of private fact. Existing precedent has tended to come down on the side of most such disclosures as newsworthy, as was the result in the press revelation that Oliver Sipple, the former marine who thwarted the assassination attempt against Gerald Ford in 1975, was gay. The law is unstable in the area of disclosure of private or semi-private facts like these, however. These scholars speculate that yet another modification of libel law since *Times v. Sullivan* may be in the wind, this one, like the *Gertz* decision, leaning toward protection of reputation and privacy and away from protection of speech and press.

Finally, what would change the way the press thinks about privacy is a shift back toward a political environment in which government is once again effective with respect to the issues that most govern our common destinies economically and socially, from deficits and industrial renewal to drugs and the fate of our cities.

If government could be made once again to work, and those in public life worked at running it (and not just at the variations on show business that politics demands),

the enormous energies of the news media would flow
back toward covering that dynamic, as they once did.
The vicious cycle would be broken—the cycle whereby
people feel alienated from intractable public issues,
politicians can find no better form of public discourse (or
policy) than to manipulate that alienation, and the press
has little to cover but the politicians' self-display, manipulative gamesmanship, and "character."

Code and Coda

There is little good, and perhaps some harm, in pin-
ning any call for a change in the journalism profession's
practice in the area of privacy to some potential disas-
trous trespass on its part or to a humbling by the Supreme Court or transformation of the American governmental system and political scene. To speak in such
terms is to acknowledge how little agreement there is
about journalistic discretion as against journalistic
valor.

The one aspect of the subject most journalists do agree
about is that the old men's club rule for covering public
officials was too passive, and that, like it or not, since
Watergate the press is in the "character cop" business.

Sociologists of police work, such as James Q. Wilson,
speak of the nuance and ambiguity inherent in the job as
between *keeping the peace* and *enforcing the law*. The
policeman as peacekeeper will wink at occasional breaches
of the law—the unauthorized opening of a fire hydrant
on a sweltering day—in the interest of preserving the
fabric of the neighborhood in time of tension. The policeman as enforcer will observe the letter of the laws even if
it inflames the neighborhood.

Here, perhaps, is a clue as to how we in the profession
and at journalism schools might similarly think about

deepening and more carefully defining the journalist's job description in the coverage of issues that impinge on privacy. The goal would be to acknowledge and confront, rather than evade or deny, the kinds of ambiguity discussed here.

Good and well-trained policemen are measured in their use of force. Overkill can backfire; timing is everything. Journalists who dig the dirt and dish it indiscriminately, rejecting discretion as "elitist" and disclaiming moral responsibility or ethical consideration because our business is simply and solely the facts, become something of a law unto themselves. *The Miami Herald* with its stakeout, followed by Paul Taylor of *The Washington Post* with his question, "Have you ever committed adultery?" and his justification later, "What I did was ask Gary Hart the question he asked for," followed by the *Post*'s role in Hart's decision to abandon his candidacy, dramatized all at once the press in the roles of investigator, prosecutor, jury, judge, and exorcist, and it was not a pretty sight. (*See How They Run*, pp. 51, 70.)

It is one thing for a decorated, battle-scarred veteran of many journalistic engagements to recite the code and let fly the chips. Ben Bradlee is the model. "There was no *anti* in me," he said of his role in the Hart case, according to Richard Ben Cramer. "I just come to work with an empty bucket. And someone fills it up every day. That day, it happened to be Hart." (*What It Takes*, p. 165.)

But that model does not come with guidance in a pinch to the less experienced, less intuitively gifted journalist. According to Taylor's own account of the Hart episode, Bradlee was quizzing him back at the office the day after the fateful Q & A with Gary Hart: "You were the one who asked that question?" said Bradlee.

"'Yeah,' I said, half expecting a high-five.

"Bradlee rolled his eyes and said, 'Shee-yit!'

"As eye rolls go, this one was ambiguous—conveying surprise more than approval or disapproval. Or so I'd like to think. I've made it a point not to ask." (*See How They Run*, p. 59.)

Ben Bradlee is a fine journalist, one who has been at the center of every major shift in the balance of power between press and politician since he covered his friend Jack Kennedy, swearing afterwards never to become close to such a figure again. By Taylor's own account and many others, Bradlee understands what his reporter did not about the ambiguities of situational ethics and about the place of discretion. When those who do not understand such matters, who are not concerned with them, move into the territory of privacy, into the riddle of the innermost self of another, more than "just the facts" are involved and words take on the firepower of actions, for there we have arrived at the privileged question of our ultimate worth as human beings, a question that used to be reserved less for each other than for our gods.

READING LIPS AND BITING SOUND: THE ETHICS OF CAMPAIGN COMMUNICATIONS

by

Royce Hanson

Royce Hanson

Royce Hanson is the Dean of the School of Social Sciences at The University of Texas at Dallas.

Dean Hanson's interest in political campaigns began in childhood, observing his father campaign for local politicians. At Central Oklahoma University, he was active as a barnstormer for gubernatorial and senatorial candidates, canvassing small towns across the state. By the time he had graduated, he had managed his roommate's successful campaign for a seat in the state legislature and organized young voters for the state party in the 1952 presidential campaign. In 1954, he served as publicity director for a gubernatorial candidate.

While completing his doctorate in Government and Public Administration at The American University, Dean Hanson became active in Maryland politics, managing the campaign of a friend for a judgeship. In 1964 and 1966, while teaching about parties and elections at The American University, Hanson was himself a candidate for office, as a Democratic nominee for Congress. He also led the successful legal and political campaign for reapportionment of the Maryland General Assembly.

Aside from his avocation in politics, Royce Hanson has pursued a successful academic and public career. Before becoming dean of the School of Social Sciences at The University of Texas at Dallas, he taught at The American University's School of Government and Public Administration. He also served as President of the Washington Center for Metropolitan Studies; Director of the New Communities Study Center of Virginia Polytechnic Institute; Chairman of the Montgomery County, Maryland, Planning Board; Staff Director of the Committee on National Urban Policy of the National Research Council; and Associate Dean of the Hubert H. Humphrey Institute of Public Affairs of the University of Minnesota. Dean Hanson is the author of many books and articles, including Tribune of the People: The Minnesota Legislature and Its Leadership; Rethinking Urban Policy: Urban Development in an Advanced Economy; *and* The Political Thicket: Reapportionment and Constitutional Government. *In addition to a Ph.D. in Government and Public Administration, he holds a law degree and is a member of the Bar of Maryland. He is a Fellow of the National Academy of Public Administration.*

READING LIPS AND BITING SOUND: THE ETHICS OF CAMPAIGN COMMUNICATIONS

by

Royce Hanson

The recent presidential campaign and our long political history notwithstanding, campaign ethics is not an oxymoron. Campaigns present unique and difficult ethical problems for both candidates and voters. Candidates face the dilemma of acting ethically and losing to someone less bothered by such niceties. Voters are too often presented with a choice between a candidate they regard as unethical and one they see as incompetent. I recall a Maryland gubernatorial primary in which the choices were characterized as a crook, an idiot, and a madman.

Ethics involves a balancing of important moral principles and interests. Understanding the ethical issues involved in campaign communications requires comprehension of the conflicting obligations and interests that impinge on decisions that campaigners must make. Such matters are rarely resolved by categorical rules.

War and Democracy

Different kinds of human activity are governed by different kinds of moral principles. Campaigning draws on the moral principles and metaphors of war and democratic governance.

Campaigns are surrogates for civil war. They substitute ballots for bullets. The vocabulary of a campaign is rich in the language of warfare—victory and defeat, attack and counterattack, strategy and tactics, rallying the troops. It is infused with moral righteousness, indignation, and belligerence. In politics as in war, there is no substitute for victory. "Politics," said Mr. Dooley, "ain't beanbag." Coming in second does not count. There are no moral victories. Unlike the vanquished in war, losers in politics sometimes do get to write the history. They also appear on talk shows or give lectures.

In war, many ordinary ethical constraints are relaxed. It is not unethical to mislead the enemy through outright lies and disinformation or to withhold information from one's own soldiers and citizens to protect lives or to achieve a strategic goal. Spying, espionage, and sabotage are regarded as necessary.

Democracy is governed by different ethical principles. It depends on the ability of voters to make informed choices about who will govern them. Since the ability to make informed choices depends upon the quality of the information the voters receive, the ethics of democracy demand that the information provided have enough integrity to allow voters to make the fundamental decision about who should govern.

Democracy is only idealistic. It is not blind. It accepts that people have divergent interests, that they will not always be honest about their interests, that they will not always play fair or count honestly. It recognizes that an unbiased citizen is as rare as a politician devoid of ambition.

Truth is expected to emerge from the competition between candidates. Unlike trials by jury, campaigns follow no rules of evidence. No one is under oath. Everything is admissible (and deniable). The electorate is not expected to be passive and unprejudiced. Voters can have their own "facts" as well as their own opinions.

Under the rules of political engagement, we expect each party and its candidates to present a view of the world most favorable to them and most damning to their opponents. The conflict gives the people a choice and makes them ultimately sovereign. It also serves as a means of testing both the candidates and the things they say against each other and against our collective experience with politicians and policies. Ultimately, we depend upon the conflicting charges and claims of candidates and the fair-mindedness of the people, individually and collectively, to winnow truth from the cacophony of argument.

Although resigned to the presence of liars in its public debates, democracy is served best by a system of public ethics that condemns lying and secrecy as political strategies. Disinformation is dangerous to informed choice. Openness is prized even when it intrudes into private matters that arguably may be irrelevant to informed public choices. Spying—euphemistically known as opposition research—is allowable as long as it is limited to discovering truths relevant to public choice that the other side is trying to conceal or to discovering, through legal means, campaign plans or tactics of the opposition.

The Watergate scandal should teach us that spying that exceeds these levels should require special justification based on moral principle. As in all discussions of ethics, the problem is in arriving at some way of judging conduct and communications that cross the boundary.

Ethics is about justification. Justification involves more than rationalization to oneself. That is merely making excuses. Justification requires a public explanation that appeals to moral principles worthy of recognition by others. It may not be necessary that the others embrace those principles; it is only necessary that they recognize them as fairly debatable by reasonable people.

In her books *Lying: Moral Choice in Public and Private Life* (Random House, 1989) and *Secrets: On the Ethics of Concealment and Revelation* (Random House, 1979), Sissela Bok recommends the "publicity" test for those tempted to lie or withhold information. She points out, for example, that the ethical test for a secret—even a military secret—is that there must be a rationale for it that can be defended publicly on moral grounds. It is quite possible to make a public justification for lying, spying, and espionage in a war. It is far harder to come up with a public justification for such tactics in a political campaign. For those who have trouble understanding the publicity test, there is a simpler formulation, the *Washington Post* test: "Can we explain this if it is on the front page of the *Post* tomorrow morning?"

Political campaigns have another problem that does not exist for military campaigns. For generals, victory is the end. For politicians in a democracy, electoral victory is only the means of attaining the end of governing. Thus, a political campaign is ethically linked to governing through the implicit contract forged by the winning candidate's promises to the voters, given in consideration of their votes. Candidates, therefore, have ethical duties to the electorate. These duties include, at a minimum, obligations to be truthful and to address serious issues of policy that confront the public. In addition, an argument can be made that a candidate has an obligation to lay out, if not a program, at least a starting position that is grounded in a set of facts and arguments that can pass the laugh test—a reasonable public in possession of the basic information would not laugh out loud at the idea. This is not a high standard.

The ethical choices made by candidates have consequences, both for themselves and for the polity. A candidate confronted with an ethical choice, even in the heat of a campaign, is obligated to consider the effect of the choice on those who will be affected by it. Lies, distortions, and artful dodges of hard issues are not harmless. The effect on the candidate can be corrosive, especially if these tactics appear to have been successful. Apparent success can lead to increasing ease when telling the next lie. It can also lead to the support of measures that the now-elected official knows or believes to be less than beneficial or even harmful. A firm commitment made in the heat of a campaign may limit the ability to address the issue thoughtfully once in office. George Bush's only famous imperative sentence, "Read my lips: No new taxes!" stands as an example of the slippery slope on which candidates place themselves when they make unequivocal pledges to support positions that they almost certainly know will be hard to keep, or at least to back away from in light of changed circumstances.

Public cynicism is fueled by evidence that candidates and officials pander to emotions and interests, that they mislead the people deliberately in order to attain office, then betray the people's trust by failing to perform what they promised. One should ask, in trying to justify taking a campaign position at odds with one's conscience or with the facts, whether so doing, even if one is victorious, will further public distrust of the political process or of the system itself.

In the recent presidential campaign, we were told that the central question was "trust." Trust is indeed a central ethical concept of democratic politics, the fragile thread that binds the public and its government. It involves the confidence that those who seek and hold office will not intentionally do wrong or mislead the public. It requires those who would be leaders to embody the public virtues that make them worthy of being followed. Fooling the people, betraying their trust in the word of their leaders, has serious consequences for democratic governance. It breeds cynicism. Bok reminds us that the damage to trust is immense when people believe that "they all lie"—that candidates deliberately mislead them, fear addressing difficult problems, raise phony issues to divert attention from their own inadequacies, do not mean what they say, and say anything to please—or when a citizen cannot tell what to believe. When trust is absent, there is no authentic leadership. The political system is left to formalism and the exercise of raw power.

The contrast between the ethics of warfare and those of democracy makes perfect sense to the disinterested observer. For candidates and their managers, however, they pose hard dilemmas. No candidate believes that the republic will be better off if his opponent wins. None assumes that the opposition is using a civics text as a campaign manual or that it will not stoop to dirty tricks as the campaign wears on or becomes close. The challenge for the ethical candidate is to devise and pursue a winning strategy without engaging in conduct that violates the ethics of democracy. For voters, the problem is one of insisting on a standard of conduct by candidates that produces a fair fight without imposing such a prudish standard of political discourse that campaigns are as entertaining as the fine print in an insurance policy.

A Short History of Sleaze

Concern for the ethics of campaign communications is hardly new. Our political campaigns have often evoked the concern of the aesthetically sensitive and the ethically prim. Each campaign brings the condemnation that it has sunk even lower than its predecessors in terms of vilification of opponents, failure to discuss important issues, and appeals to baser instincts in the electorate. This judgment may be the result of a lack of historical perspective.

American campaigns have long been ethically challenged. In 1800, in our first seriously contested presidential election, scurrilous tales were circulated about Thomas Jefferson's "concubine" slave, Sally Hennings. John Adams was savaged as a pompous royalist, suppressor of liberty, and enemy of the people.

In the 1824 and 1828 elections, Andrew Jackson was denounced as a duelist, an adulterer, and a murderer. John Quincy Adams was subjected to a four-year campaign of unremitting vilification by the Jacksonians. A rumor was circulated throughout the country that he had misspent public money to install a billiard table in the White House for the amusement of his son.

The years leading to the Civil War, when bullets displaced the ballot as the means of settling a political dispute, were especially rich in demonization and invidious labeling. The minor Equal Rights Party was relabeled by its enemies as the Locofocos. Their rural counterpart was called the Barnburners. This moniker suggested that like the Dutch farmer who burned down his barn to get the rats out, they were willing to destroy the whole system to rid themselves of the establishment politicians of their day. The Barnburners called their adversaries the Hunkers—for their hunkering after office. The Native American Party was organized into secret gangs that terrorized Catholics and other immigrants. Because members were instructed to deny any knowledge of such goings on, Horace Greeley stuck them with the name Know-Nothings.

These parties of our golden past were no pikers in making sweeping campaign allegations or fomenting class and sectional warfare. The abolitionist Liberty Party, for example, contended that the depression of 1837 had been foisted by the "spendthrift, slaveholding South upon a frugal, industrious, and unsuspecting, free-labor North." The Know-Nothings denounced the Democratic Party as the "party of foreignism." These minor parties had in common a passion for finding scapegoats or conspiracies at the heart of the nation's problems.

In 1856, Republican campaigners focused their diatribes on "Bleeding Kansas." Republican floats in parades depicted underfed laborers and the slogan "Buchanan's workshop: Ten cents a day," suggesting that misrepresentation of the opposition's economic policies is not a new feature of American campaigns. Even "Honest Abe" Lincoln was not immune to flights of demagoguery. In one report of his 1856 speech to a Republican gathering, he was heard to suggest that "they"—the pro-slavery interests—would not be content until they had not only enslaved all Negroes but made "things" rather than persons of all white working men.

The campaign of 1884 remains a high point of low tactics in presidential campaigning. A New York divine who supported the Republican candidate, James G. Blaine, tarred the Democrats as the party of "Rum, Romanism, and Rebellion." Grover Cleveland, who confessed to fathering an illegitimate child, was satirized in the jingle, "Ma, Ma! Where's my pa? Gone to the White House, Ha, Ha, Ha!" The Democrats replied in kind, taunting "Blaine, Blaine, James G. Blaine; The continental liar from the State of Maine!" In the 1892 campaign, Cleveland was accused of beating his wife. Nineteenth-century voters, foreshadowing the lapse in family values decried a century later, elected Cleveland both times.

The acrimonious primary campaign of 1912 between President William Howard Taft and former President Theodore Roosevelt featured a rumor that Roosevelt had a drinking problem. Taft himself accused Roosevelt of Caesarism and demagoguery. Roosevelt, no slouch in the use of campaign invective, accused Taft of political chicanery and of being the candidate of "the bosses."

The 1928 campaign fostered anti-Catholic broadsides and calumny directed at Al Smith, the first Catholic nominated by a major party for the presidency. Smith was characterized as an uncouth clown, a tobacco-chewing, wife-beating drunkard who would turn the White House into a local branch of the Vatican. Rumors about Franklin Roosevelt's health were so extensively spread in 1932—including the story that he suffered from syphilis rather than infantile paralysis—that he submitted to a thorough physical examination by a board of physicians, who then publicly pronounced him in excellent health. Herbert Hoover, the man who organized the massive international relief effort at the end of World War I, was successfully depicted by Democrats as unfeeling and inept.

The Functions of Campaign Communications

Against this historical perspective, it is hard to say that campaigns have deteriorated. It is equally hard to say that our ethical standards have risen. Could it be that the problem is really not so bad? Or that however bad it is, there can be no cure that would not be worse than the affliction? I believe that the answer to both questions is no. Before suggesting what might be done, however, we should take a close look at the nature of a political campaign.

A political campaign is a propaganda contest, designed to mobilize voters to support its candidates. It is waged with growing intensity and ferocity as the election approaches. The communications involved are aimed to both saturate the consciousness of the general public and to penetrate and direct the wills of specifically targeted publics. The basic communications strategy of a campaign has four primary objectives: (1) to control the agenda of the campaign; (2) to consolidate and reinforce the support of core supporters and constituencies; (3) to convince the undecided and convert the doubtful or those inclined to oppose you; and (4) to confuse, demoralize, or refute the opposition.

A. Controlling the Agenda

The principal function of the two-party conventions in 1992 was to try to set the agenda for the presidential campaign. To do so, they sought to define the issues, their candidates, and their opponents.

At the Democratic Convention, "change" was the watchword—change in the Democratic Party and the need for change from the status quo. Within that agenda, the Democrats defined the central issue of the campaign to be the state and future of the economy. So successful were the Democrats in setting the agenda that the Republicans began to argue, however implausibly for an incumbent presidential party, that it was they who were the genuine agents of change. They sought, however, to shift the frame of the agenda to one of changing the Congress, rather than the presidency. They also used their convention to put "character" and "family values" on the agenda. Republican strategists saw these not only as issues of substantive policy but as a means of putting Governor Clinton on the defensive. They were also a means of shifting the focus of voters from the state of the economy, which was hurting President Bush and his party, to themes where the President was perceived as having an advantage.

From an ethical perspective, a campaign ought to address issues that are central to public policy and at some level to be about alternative approaches to those issues. This obligation to address serious issues with serious proposals does not, however, win elections for the party or candidate with the more vulnerable record or position. No strategist likes to fight on weak ground. The need to dominate the electoral agenda tempts candidates either to outbid their opponents or to try to outflank them. President Bush tried both tactics. He proposed an across-the-board tax cut, combined with a list of other budget management measures, as his "solution" to the economic problem. And he embraced family values and character as the central issues of the campaign.

Both tactics were ethically suspect. Although the tax cut was indeed a substantive proposal, it was conditioned on unspecified spending cuts, which were to be revealed only after Bush's reelection. A case can be made that the character of candidates is a legitimate matter of concern to voters. Its use by the Republican Party was, however, not only a vehicle for legitimately contrasting the qualities of judgment and temperament of the two presidential candidates but a device to excuse attacks on Clinton's alleged past sexual conduct and patriotism. Similarly, policy issues that affect the stability of the family are proper campaign fare. When used, as they were at the convention and afterward, to enflame religious intolerance, distort the positions of Hillary Clinton on policy matters, and sanctimoniously shanghai God into exclusive service for one political party, the boundary was crossed from fair debate about policy into the unethical invention of phony issues.

There is no ethical difference between "Rum, Romanism, and Rebellion" and Congressman Newt Gingrich's slur that Woody Allen's nonincest with his nondaughter of his nonmarriage perfectly fit the values of the Democratic Party. It is inconceivable that a reasonable public would approve in advance the use of such strategies if those strategies were explained to them. It is difficult to see how such issues advance the ability of voters to make informed choices.

Subtle distinctions do not help voters make up their minds. Thus, candidates often resort to exaggeration of their differences to polarize the electorate. As the 1992 campaign drew to a close, the President, who based his claim of being the environmental president on the Clean Air Act, repeatedly referred to Senator Albert Gore, the Democratic candidate for vice president, as "the Ozone Man." He attacked Gore as an environmental extremist, asserting that if Clinton and Gore were elected, the country would be overrun with owls, but there would be no jobs.

Another way of dividing the electorate is to accuse one's opponent of being a tool of some sinister or unpopular group. In the recent campaign, Governor Clinton made repeated references to President Bush's "rich friends." The Bush campaign attacked Clinton as being a tool of the trial lawyers. Jerry Brown in the Democratic primaries and Ross Perot in the general election regularly charged that their opponents were tools of the special interest political action committees and the "tasseled loafer lobbyists."

The beauty of the "tool of ___" issue is that it can be refuted only at the risk of possible alienation of a significant supporter. As propaganda, the tool charge works off stereotypes, evokes fear, usually oversimplifies the facts, and best of all, tends to stick to the opponent. In 1940, Harold Ickes' characterization of Wendell Willkie as Wall Street's barefoot boy was devastating. In a few cases, candidates may indeed be tools of special interests, and such charges are justifiable. In others, the charge is pure hokum. In such cases, the campaign making the charge is perpetrating a fraud on the voters. There is no moral justification for such behavior.

B. Consolidating and Reinforcing the Base

A successful campaign must have a devoted and zealous core of believers who will persist against all odds, ignore all their candidate's flaws, and proselytize without mercy. Like a conquering army, this hard core of supporters feeds on success; each victory refreshes its adrenalin and intensifies loyalty.

The core constituency feeds on the myths of factional purity, party purpose, leader nobility, and the perfidy of the opposition. Because the President was perceived as being on shaky ground with basic core factions of the Republican Party, the national convention devoted much of its program, and the President gave over much of his acceptance address, to shoring up his base. Former President Ronald Reagan called the faithful to endorse Bush. Presidential candidate Patrick Buchanan declared cultural war on the Democrats. The platform was dominated by the favorite issues of the Republican Right, and an entire day of the program was devoted to "family values." Richard Bond, the party chairman, told a reporter, "We are America. The Democrats are not America." Bush apologized for raising taxes and pledged to cut them if returned to power. He was saying the things hard-core partisans longed to hear.

For the hard core of supporters, the emphasis of the message tends to be hard-edged, ideological, and drawn in terms of stark alternatives. The morale of the "troops" is a constant concern. The opposition is the "enemy camp." Debates are characterized as "battles," and great emphasis is placed on winning and losing these and other propaganda battles. The opposition candidate's camp is demonized, as is the candidate. All of this reinforcing communication is calculated to motivate workers and to keep them inspired throughout the campaign.

Although the Clinton-Gore bus trips were aimed at the general electorate, a primary mission was also to fire up the core support of the party, to create in its constituencies a sense of thrust and excitement. Campaign appearances are important not only because they give candidates an opportunity to communicate with voters but primarily because preparing for a major appearance by a presidential candidate requires the activation of the local party faithful. It energizes them to commit time and effort to proselytizing their neighbors.

C. Conversion

The third objective of campaign communications strategy is to convince the undecided and convert voters initially inclined to vote for others or not to vote at all. The skeptical, the alienated, the undecided, the inattentive, and the hostile represent different target groups for whom different propaganda approaches are needed.

Such appeals occasionally bump into communications aimed at consolidating the base and require special attention and communications skills. Clinton's campaign rested substantially on a conversion stratagem: From the beginning of his primary effort, he was signaling voters who had, for six of the past seven elections, voted for Republican or third-party candidates—blue collar, ethnic, and middle-class white voters—that he was a "different kind" of Democrat, one who had their interests at heart. While moderating the Democratic image and message to gain converts, Clinton had to maintain the enthusiasm of the hard core of more ideological Democratic voters and keep intact his support among minorities. He made healing racial and social divisions a central theme of his primary and general election campaigns, while preaching a joint message of help and responsibility. Help appealed to his core constituencies, responsibility to potential converts. In a Dallas television appearance, Clinton used a question from a reporter about a complaint from Jesse Jackson that he was ignoring the base of the Democratic Party to assert that by opening the front door to those who had not recently supported the party, he was not pushing anyone out the back door.

Conversion involves both positive and negative appeals. Usually, the early stages of a campaign are devoted to positive appeals to voters, introducing the candidate and his or her ideas, values, and positions. The aim is to "define" the candidate and the campaign in a manner that is impregnable to assault. It is a period of image building designed to both consolidate support and lay a base for converting voters initially undecided or disposed to prefer others.

It is not always possible, however, to maintain a positive campaign, notwithstanding the virtuous claims of every candidate to stay on the high road. In the competitive world of politics, the high road is generally reserved for the few candidates who do not have serious challengers.

Negative campaigning is an almost essential aspect of the conversion stratagem in campaigning, because a convert's vote counts twice as much as one you already have. In recent campaigns, no conversion stratagem has been more effective than the propaganda war waged against Michael Dukakis in 1988. Dukakis had carefully burnished his positive image as a hands-on, innovative, "competent" leader who was raised up from immigrant roots to serve the people, fulfilling the American Dream.

Bush started the campaign with high negative reactions in opinion polls. He was seen as weak and vacillating, as fairly devoid of deep convictions, and as an unconvincing successor to Ronald Reagan, "The Great Communicator." Bush was far behind Dukakis in the preference polls when the Democratic Convention ended, and a subject of some ridicule.

In deciding on a strategy to convert voters from support of Dukakis, or at least from indifference to either candidate, the Bush campaign sought to redefine not only Dukakis but Bush. It set out to undermine the Dukakis image, to make him appear incompetent, unpatriotic, and soft on crime. In the process, Bush would appear competent, patriotic, and hard on crime.

By almost any standard, the Bush campaign was as unethical as it was successful. It calculatedly misrepresented Dukakis's record and positions. Without doubt, Dukakis's failure to respond to attacks with dispatch contributed to his undoing and even compounded the image of him that the Bush campaign was trying to create. In the process, it successfully converted likely Dukakis voters to Bush voters or persuaded them not to vote.

Three episodes from the Bush campaign illustrate the ethical problems that can easily afflict conversion tactics. Bush's boat ride in Boston Harbor dramatized the fact that in spite of Dukakis's claim to support environmental programs, he had not cleaned up his own harbor. What Bush did not say, of course, was that the delays were exacerbated by Reagan administration reductions in funding for water pollution control programs or that in spite of lack of federal support, Dukakis was implementing an aggressive state cleanup program.

The Harbor television ad was effective because it was a bold challenge to an opponent on his own turf, showing that Bush was no wimp. It was also effective because, although the charge was simple, refutation required a more complicated argument than could be presented in a thirty-second soundbite. Perhaps the greatest reason for its effectiveness was that the image conveyed by television was so powerful that almost no set of mere words could expunge it.

The second line of the Bush campaign to redefine Dukakis and convert voters inclined to favor him was to attack his patriotism. This was done through the flag stunts. Dukakis had vetoed a bill enacted by the Massachusetts General Court to require teachers to lead students in recitation of the Pledge of Allegiance at the start of each school day. Dukakis vetoed the bill on the advice of counsel that it was unconstitutional. Bush assailed his opponent on the veto, asserting that he would have signed the bill and implying that the governor did not sign because he was a "liberal" who did not respect the values dear to the American people and did not love the grand old flag.

Bush used innuendo in his appearance before the Veterans of Foreign Wars Convention to raise further doubts about Dukakis's patriotism. Under fire for his selection of Dan Quayle as his running mate because of questions concerning Quayle's enlistment in the National Guard during the Vietnam War, Bush declared that Quayle "did not go to Canada, he did not burn his draft card, and he damn sure didn't burn the American flag." The next day, Republican Senator Steve Syms told reporters that he had heard there was a picture somewhere of Kitty Dukakis, the Democratic nominee's wife, burning an American flag. Although completely untrue, this story circulated for several days, adding to the image of Dukakis as an enemy of the flag. Bush burnished the contrast between himself and Dukakis, appearing at a flag factory and denouncing his opponent for being a "card carrying" member of the American Civil Liberties Union.

By far the most devastating of the Bush attacks on Dukakis, however, were the revolving door and Willie Horton ads. The first, run by the Bush campaign itself, showed a prison guard standing helplessly by as prisoners marched through a revolving barred gate. On the screen, a legend told viewers that Dukakis's "revolving door prison policy gave weekend furloughs to first-degree murderers not eligible for parole. . . . Now, Michael Dukakis says he wants to do for America what he did for Massachusetts. America can't afford that risk." An independent campaign committee actually produced the infamous Willie Horton ad, which showed a mug shot of the African-American murderer who raped a white woman in Maryland while on furlough from the Massachusetts penitentiary.

Reporters Jack Germond and Jules Witcover summed up the 1988 campaign as the "most mean-spirited and negative campaign in modern-day American political history. "Bush's managers offered one principal excuse for their campaign strategy. It was the only way they could get on the evening news. The line of defense seemed to be, it's not our fault, the media made us do it. "[T]he concept of campaign as educational exercise," wrote Germond and Witcover, "crumbled before the concept of campaign as warfare, and Dukakis was gunned down in the process." (*Whose Broad Stripes and Bright Stars: The Trivial Pursuit of the Presidency 1988*, Warner Books, 1989, p. 458.)

The ethical question here is whether the excuse offered is an acceptable justification for the strategy. It is not. If spelled out publicly, it would say, in effect, that we are going to falsify our opponent's record, distort fact, use innuendo based on a lie to vilify his character, and decline to denounce propaganda that appears to appeal to racial fears. The need to get on the evening news is an excuse that does not address the substance of the charge against the campaign.

But they won. Are these tactics justifiable if indeed the country was better off with Bush than Dukakis in the White House? Again, it seems to me that the answer has to be no. First, there is no evidence that such tactics were necessary, and certainly none that a Dukakis administration would have been worse for the country. There is no way of proving that one way or the other. Second, the negative campaign against Dukakis apparently contributed to public cynicism about politics and the political process. An argument might be made that the egregious nature of the Bush campaign has been so much discussed that it has led to public revulsion at negative tactics and that it, therefore, might be justified as a necessary lesson for democracy. Unfortunately, only fragmentary evidence exists that negative campaigning hurts its perpetrator. In 1992, the negative ads in senatorial primaries in Illinois and New York appear to have backfired, contributing to the defeat of their authors. They also contributed to the defeat of their targets. Só the practical lesson is that negative ads work, just not always as they are supposed to.

Again in 1992, the dominant stratagem of the Bush campaign was a concerted negative attack on Bill Clinton's "character." By the time of the presidential debates, the Republican strategy had narrowed to an attempt to portray Clinton as untrustworthy. Both the President and his campaign surrogates attacked Clinton's statements on issues and, especially, his explanations of his draft status as demonstrations of his "waffling." Vice President Quayle, in the debates, was blunter: "Bill Clinton has trouble telling the truth," he charged, over and over again. The Clinton campaign countered by pointing to Bush's reversals of his tax pledge and capitalizing on reports of former Defense Secretary Casper Weinberger's diary that contradicted Bush's claim to have been "out of the loop" on the arms-for-hostages deal with Iran. The trust issue succeeded in driving up negative perceptions of Clinton. It ultimately backfired on Bush, but only because of his vulnerability on the tax pledge and the arms-for-hostages deal.

These negative attacks, however unpleasant they were for the contenders and for the public, were not entirely out of ethical bounds. The public has a legitimate interest in the integrity of its leaders. Although it is not incumbent on candidates to point to inconsistencies, dissembling, and trimming by their adversaries, neither is it unethical, as long as their criticisms are subject to reasonable proofs.

In two notable instances, negative campaigning in

1992 failed to meet even this low standard. Shortly before the first presidential debate, a group of right-wing Republican congressmen began a series of attacks on Clinton. Admitting they had no proof, they alleged that while a student at Oxford, Clinton had traveled to Moscow as an invitee of the KGB. They also alleged that Clinton had been a major organizer of demonstrations in London against U.S. Vietnam War policy. The juxtaposition of these charges carried the clear inference that Clinton had been disloyal and that he was trying to cover it up.

After a meeting with the congressmen at the White House, Bush used a Larry King show interview to say that although he did not have the facts, he was "troubled" by reports of Clinton's Moscow visit just a year after the Soviet crushing of the "Prague Spring" movement in Czechoslovakia and with the idea of demonstrating against "your country" in a foreign land. He said that Clinton should "come clean" about these activities.

As press investigations demonstrated that Clinton's Moscow trip was innocuous and that his role in the London demonstrations was minor, the President backed off the innuendo that Clinton was somehow a Red agent or Communist sympathizer, but he continued to hammer on the thought that demonstrations "against his country when American boys were dying" were unpatriotic. Clinton, in the first debate, charged Bush with McCarthy-style tactics and pointedly reminded the President that his father, when in the U.S. Senate, had opposed McCarthy, whom the elder Bush had voted to censure for his unsupported allegations of Communist influence or affiliations.

The Bush campaign sank deeper in its ethical quagmire when it was revealed that political officials in the

State Department had searched Clinton's passport file, apparently seeking information to discredit him. Initially, the Department insisted that its examination was a "routine" response to a press inquiry, but the Acting Secretary of State reversed that position and the matter was turned over to the department's inspector general for an investigation. Then a report was leaked to the *Washington Post* (remember the publicity test!) that the same officials had looked into the file of Clinton's mother! After the election, it was revealed that the same officials had examined Ross Perot's file and removed papers from it.

The second great ethical lapse of the campaign was Perot's statement, nine days before the election, that the real reason he had withdrawn from the campaign in July was that he had received information that the Bush campaign planned to smear his daughter with a faked photograph and to disrupt her wedding, scheduled for the next month. Having made the allegation, and admitting that he could not prove it, Perot then told his supporters to "forget it." He refused to identify his sources. The FBI, which had investigated the charges at Perot's request, stated that it could find no evidence to support them.

The ethical implications of the Perot story are enormous. First of all, he was telling his supporters and the general public that when he withdrew in July, he had misrepresented his reasons. He implicitly argued that the withholding of information was justified to protect another. But that justification requires the belief that the lie is necessary because there is no reasonable alternative to protect the other person from harm.

The obligation to tell the truth is greater for a public figure than for a private person. Perot's July statement met neither a personal nor a public standard for justification. By concealing his real reason for withdrawing, he misled his supporters and the public. If he intended to reenter the race, as sometimes he implied that he did, he lied about his intentions as well as his motivations. It is hard to reconcile such behavior with the publicity test: Would a reasonable public have thought them morally defensible if explained in advance?

If Perot had a credible basis for believing the dirty tricks story, he had an obligation to expose it. If he did not, he had an obligation not to use it as a basis for a public action. Finally, alternatives were available. He could have publicly denounced such tactics, in general terms if he had no hard evidence and in specific terms if he did. Such a preemptive strike would have made any real conspiracy against his family nonviable. In addition to his own ample security arrangements for the wedding, his family would have been entitled to Secret Service protection.

CBS appears to have been aware of the rumor about the dirty tricks before Perot made his public statement, but the producer of *60 Minutes* stated that without Perot making the charge publicly, they would have had no story, because they could find no evidence to support it. Even giving Perot the benefit of the doubt that *he* believed the story initially, he knew at the time he went public with it that there was no supporting evidence. He asserted an unprovable statement that could also not be disproved. Then he asked the public to "forget it." This is like handing a small boy a box of matches and saying, "Now don't play with them." He accused an opponent of conspiring to commit a heinous act and cast himself as a victim of an outrageous abuse of power.

Although initially some polls showed that more people believed Perot than Bush's denials, the salvo lodged firmly in Perot's foot. It gave the Bush campaign the opportunity to raise questions about Perot's character, calling attention to his alleged fondness for conspiracy theories and to his temperament, judgment, and erratic political behavior. Bush's press secretary, Marvin Fitzwater, bit sound, calling Perot "paranoid." An ethical question may also be raised by this unlicensed practice of psychiatry.

D. Confusing the Opposition

A substantial portion of a campaign's propaganda is aimed at neither supporters nor the undecided but at the opposition. Its purpose is to sow confusion, distrust, and doubt of victory.

Some communications are aimed directly at the opposing candidate. They may reinforce support for the attacker among supporters, but their principal objective is to rattle the target, throw him or her off stride, or cause embarrassment. Perhaps the finest illustration of this technique is Franklin D. Roosevelt's "Fala" speech in 1944. Roosevelt maintained a "presidential" posture, refraining from active campaigning until late October. In the meantime, the Republican candidate, Thomas E. Dewey, was darting about the country, denouncing Roosevelt as a dictator, a destroyer of free enterprise, and a tired old man. A whispering campaign was mounted about Roosevelt's health, the Red scare, the war service of his sons, and the morale-building trips of his wife. Roosevelt's strategists felt that the President needed to make a strong speech to rally the Democrats and gain the offensive. They also felt that the one thing Dewey would not be able to take was ridicule.

In a speech before the Teamsters Union, Roosevelt began, "Well here we are together again—after four years—and what years they have been. I am actually four years older—which seems to annoy some people." Accusing the Republicans of practicing the Big Lie when they accused the Democrats of being responsible for the Great Depression and World War II, he then went on:

> "The Republican leaders have not been content to make personal attacks upon me—or my wife—or my sons—they now include my little dog, Fala. Unlike the members of my family, Fala resents this. When he learned that the Republican fiction writers had concocted a story that I had left him behind on an Aleutian Island and had sent a destroyer back to find him—at a cost to the taxpayer of two or three, or eight or twenty million dollars—his Scotch soul was furious. He has not been the same dog since. I am accustomed to hearing malicious falsehoods about myself but I think I have a right to object to libelous statements about my dog." (Harold F. Gosnell, *Champion Campaigner: Franklin D. Roosevelt*, Macmillan Co., 1952, pp. 205-206.)

The widely circulated Democratic story then became that the American people preferred a big man with a little dog to a little man with a big dog. Roosevelt had shifted the campaign from one of Dewey against the President to Dewey versus Fala. As expected, the speech made Dewey furious. He retaliated in a shrill attack on Roosevelt, which left the impression that Dewey was mean spirited and humorless.

Is ridicule within the bounds of ethical campaigning? It is so much fun, it is hard to argue that it is not. Humor and ridicule directed at one's opponent are generally ethically acceptable, within the rough rules of campaigning. Surely Senator Paul Wellstone's brilliant "Looking for Rudy" TV ad in 1992 addressed a legitimate campaign issue—the refusal of Minnésota Senator Rudy Boschwicz to debate or discuss the issues of the campaign. The ad put Boschwicz on the defensive and contributed substantially to his defeat. It was not particularly mean spirited. Senator Lloyd Bentsen's rejoinder to Dan Quayle during the 1988 vice presidential debate, "Senator, you're no Jack Kennedy!" not only put Quayle off stride, it crystallized a major concern of the campaign—Quayle's qualifications for the office for which he had been nominated.

Humor and even ridicule are legitimate forms of campaign propaganda, as long as they are within the bounds of debatable taste and a reasonable public could accept them as morally defensible. The Republican ad of 1988 showing the helmeted and bobbing head of Michael Dukakis in his celebrated tank ride was in itself not unfair comment. As a general rule, candidates are grown people. It is usually their own foibles of character and conduct that make them targets of ridicule. It is natural, even healthy, to laugh at vain people who allow themselves to be photographed in silly hats.

One element that should be kept in mind in judging the ethics of campaign attacks is that there is another candidate who has both an interest in exposing the shams of the opposition and a responsibility to do so. This allows wider latitude to language that could be unethical in the hands of a propaganda monopoly. There are, however, limits to what competition can correct. All opponents are not equal in resources and propaganda skills. Occasions arise in which both sides devote their energies to misrepresentations, exaggerations, and demagoguery. Those who seek office owe the democracy better. Even when we can count on competition to help us discover truth, the basic rules of ethical discourse should apply. It should be possible to make a fairly debatable public defense, on moral grounds, of the use of any communication.

Reconciling Political Necessity and Ethical Justification

From the candidate's perspective, the function of a campaign is to get elected. Any campaign communication is wasted if it does not contribute to that result. In an ideal campaign, the candidate utters no sound and makes no appearance, campaign ads and literature contain no language or symbols, paraphernalia and events stimulate no impulse, that does not contribute to that end.

The most effective campaign communications carry two messages simultaneously at different levels. One message is substantive, addressing some issue of the campaign. The other is symbolic, designed to convey an impression of the candidate as a superior leader—gifted, brilliant, tough, dynamic, wise, prudent, experienced, and humane. Like good oratory, effective campaign communication appeals to both the mind and the heart; it informs and motivates.

A. Symbols

From a societal perspective, the function of campaigns is to crystallize choices so that voters can make an informed selection among the alternatives offered them. Campaign communication is, therefore, rich in symbols. Campaign colors are chosen with great care to convey an image of patriotism (red, white, and blue), care for the environment (green), or energy and intensity (red and white). Flags are ubiquitous, if not an issue themselves, as in 1988. Television ads depict sturdy workers, happy children, small towns, and majestic scenery. Patriotism, a refuge for scoundrels even more secure than the Scriptures, is celebrated through parades and speeches that wander purposefully through the nation's pantheon of wars and heroes. A candidate's war wounds, if any, are displayed and recounted.

Candidates tend, in campaign literature and advertisements, to be portrayed in heroic terms. Their public virtues—honesty, intelligence, seriousness of purpose, humanity, humor, fidelity to causes and family, and accomplishments—are lionized. Praise is documented by stories of struggle and perseverance, of leadership, of steadiness in crisis, of accomplishment against the odds. We are served a Bill Clinton who never knew his father, the victim of an auto accident; who grew up in a small town, where he had to walk to the outhouse; who fought off an abusive and alcoholic stepfather; and who improved himself in spite of all the odds to become a model student, a Rhodes Scholar, a governor revered by his peers. President Bush was presented as a youthful war hero, an enterprising business executive, a public servant propelled by ability through the chairs of power, the great world leader, the scourge of Saddam Hussein, the presiding genius of the fall of communism, and the guardian of family values.

It is fair to say that these were not balanced portraits of two political careerists. Their point was to associate the candidate with symbolic virtues that give voters clues to their character and their capacity for the presidency. It is hard to say that either portrait was unethical in a political system that depends on the opposition to pick out and publicize flaws, and one in which there is widespread recognition that much of political communication is hyperbole if not sheer bunkum.

B. *Endorsements*

Candidates also seek endorsements of groups and prominent individuals, political leaders, and celebrities. Association with party, group, and leaders provides an important cue for voters. They tell us whether the candidate is likely to fit into a particular political faction or tradition and suggest whether he or she will be a team player or a solo performer.

When the head of the ticket is popular, candidates for lesser offices virtually submerge themselves in the mantle of the leader. This tactic is known in campaign lore as Shorenstein's Law. According to the story, Shorenstein was a Tammany sachem responsible for preparing the campaign literature of down-ballot candidates in the 1936 general election. One candidate for Surrogate, a minor New York judicial office, was outraged when he discovered that his name was not even on the literature. He burst into Shorenstein's clubhouse, demanded to see the boss, and asked how he was expected to get elected if his name wasn't even on the party literature. "The only name and picture here is Roosevelt!" he shouted.

Shorenstein calmly told the angry hack that he was not on the literature because Shorenstein's Law had been applied to the preparation of all campaign materials.

"What the hell is Shorenstein's Law?" the wannabe implored.

"Come with me and I will explain it for you," said Shorenstein.

They left the office, got on the subway, and rode to the Battery, where they walked to the ferry landing from

Staten Island. As a boat began its docking procedure, Shorenstein pointed and asked, "What do you see happening here?"

"Well," the candidate replied, "I see the big ship coming into the harbor, and as it does, it is sucking up all the crud that was in the water and carrying it in with it."

"That," the sachem confided, "is Shorenstein's Law, and that is why Roosevelt is on your literature."

Sometimes, of course, candidates are carried away by endorsing up—associating themselves with their party leader. My 1964 campaign literature asserted that "President Johnson Needs Royce Hanson in Congress," implying that LBJ would probably be stymied in achieving the Great Society without my presence. I probably got what I deserved for this bit of hyperbole when, at a rally in that campaign, LBJ introduced me as "that great Democrat, my good friend, George Hanson."

When the top of the ticket is less popular, disassociation—either silently or loudly—is not uncommon. I can recall a Democratic congressional candidate on Maryland's eastern shore—George Wallace country in 1964—running under the slogan, "Your Kind of Democrat!"

C. *Issues and Themes*

Issues give voters cues about what the candidates might do if elected and whether they are sympathetic to the concerns of various interests. In a pluralistic nation like the United States, with a federated electoral system for choosing a President, a successful campaign strategy requires a complex structure of issues for a campaign. Since the name of the game is getting elected, and getting elected requires a majority of votes in the electoral college, the issues spread offered by a candidate must be rich enough to appeal to constituencies capable of coalescing into majorities in states as diverse as New York, Illinois, Texas, California, Florida, Michigan, and North Carolina. Each party can calculate differently, but there are enough states in which they must contest head-on that it is not surprising that candidates and their managers prefer to err on the side of ambiguity on some issues to leave themselves wiggle room as the campaign unfolds.

Clear-cut positions on issues can trap candidates in postures that are vulnerable to attack. Appeals to one group may foster disenchantment in others. Because of such problems, campaign managers and candidates alike often prefer to develop symbolic "themes" for a campaign rather than a portfolio of issues. Themes are more ephemeral than positions, thus harder to attack directly. In addition, voters who would disagree on issues can read into themes almost anything they like. Themes also have the virtue of capturing the underlying mood of the electorate, whereas issues, which are inherently polarizing, cannot do so.

Successful campaign themes are hard to oppose but automatically place the opposition on the defensive. That is why "change" and "trust" were so attractive to Democrats and Republicans, respectively, in 1992. Unsuccessful themes put their advocate on the defensive; they require an explanation. Explanations, of course, lead to the taking of positions on issues, which divide constituencies rather than merge them.

A 1983 memo by campaign adviser Bernard Aronson to Democratic presidential candidate Walter Mondale captures well the importance of a campaign theme to the propaganda strategy of the candidate:

> "Every winning candidate in recent history has crystallized the message of his candidacy in a

Speech. . . . The Speech is a statement of hope; an evocation of basic American values and idealism; a celebration of American possibilities; a summoning up of the energies of the nation to meet a challenge, and a call to action. It's a distillation of the candidate's message—the themes that make the American people wish to march behind the candidate's leadership in the direction he would lead." (Peter Goldman and Tony Fuller, *The Quest for the Presidency*, Bantam, 1985, p. 387.)

In a similar vein, presidential assistant Richard Darman wrote in 1984 to President Reagan's managers:

"Paint RR as the personification of all that is right with, or heroized by, America. Leave Mondale in a position where an attack on Reagan is tantamount to an attack on America's idealized image of itself—where a vote against Reagan is, in some subliminal sense, a vote against a mythic 'AMERICA.'" (*Id.*, p. 413.)

Campaign themes are wars of metaphors: "The Cross of Gold," "We stand at Armageddon," "A New Deal," "The New Frontier," "Getting Government Off Our Backs," "the crazy aunt in the basement." The ethical questions they raise center on the extent to which the chosen metaphors fairly encapsulate what a candidacy is about and provide authentic cues to how he or she might perform, if elected.

D. Promises

The campaign promise has a bad reputation. Some of it is not deserved. Democracy demands promises from its would-be leaders. Promises are one of the prices voters extract from candidates for their support. Through promises, a candidate manufactures her own mandate for action once elected. And promises provide one of the yardsticks against which voters can measure the performance of incumbents: Did they do what they promised?

In theory, at least, an election seals a covenant between voters and those whom they elect. Voters agree to allow the people they elect to govern them for a limited time, but the legitimacy of their power rests on maintenance of a trust, rather than on an agency relationship with the public. In this sense, a campaign promise should not always be binding. The concept of public office as a public trust requires that an official act in the interest of the public, even if it means abandoning a prior promise. Circumstances may vitiate promises made in good faith. Thus, a sincere promise not to engage in war does not bind a President to refuse to defend the nation against invasion. The ethics of trusteeship, however, demand that, if a promise cannot be kept, the public is owed a justification for the change in policy.

Unkept or broken promises can be embarrassing. In the 1932 campaign, Roosevelt promised in a speech in Pittsburgh that if elected, he would balance the budget. When he realized, after becoming President, that balancing the budget would be impossible and unwise if he was to fight the depression effectively, Roosevelt was nonetheless beleaguered by his opponents for going back on a solemn promise. According to legend, he asked Sam Rosenman, his speech writer, if it was true that he had made such a promise.

"Yes, sir," Rosenman replied, "you sure did. In Pittsburgh."

"Well," Roosevelt asked, "what do you think I should do about it?"

"There are three possibilities," Rosenman suggested. "You can say you never said it. You can say you were misquoted. Or, you can say you have never been in Pittsburgh."

He might have added a piece of general advice: Don't make promises that have a high likelihood of coming back to haunt you.

There are no ethical problems with promises that are made in good faith and based on current knowledge but turn out to be unfulfillable, as long as the reasons for failure are explained, also in good faith. There *is* an ethical problem with promises that are made in good faith but in ignorance of the facts, because candidates have an obligation to know what they are talking about so they do not mislead voters. Promises that are made with knowledge that they are likely to be unfulfilled are clearly unethical. They are lies and cannot be justified on any grounds other than the argument that they will help the candidate get elected.

E. Pandering, Dodges, Hedges, and Straddles

Candidates aim to please. With the possible exception of former Texas Governor Bill Clements, no one ever got elected by insulting people. Candidates are tempted to say what their audience wants to hear. The ethical issue is whether the person who is making promises the audience wants to hear is honestly stating his views on the issues or is parroting without conviction a line he knows will be received favorably.

Since some groups hold directly opposing views on some subjects, candidates must sometimes choose to make promises that will gain them support from one side of an issue but earn the enmity of groups on the other side. The dilemma for the ethical candidate is that the promises made in a campaign to aggregate enough votes to win may make it impossible to govern once the election has been won.

One way in which candidates try to avoid this trap is to emphasize broad "valence" issues—issues that invoke broad consensus values but do not require commitment to specific positions. "Family values" is a valence issue. No one is against family values. It is a phrase that allows the person hearing it to pour into it her own policy preferences. The difficulty with valence issues is that they provide virtually no mandate for action once an election has been won. The victor's constituency may be deeply divided over specific policies to advance something as amorphous as family values.

Straddling sensitive issues is a technique of maintaining an electoral coalition, composed of groups who support a candidate for different reasons. Hedging or straddling ceases being ethically justifiable when a candidate knows that revealing his true position would cause a significant number of voters to desert him. Although it is not necessary for a candidate to reveal everything he thinks about every potential issue, it is important for the public to know about positions on issues that have been raised in the campaign. Thus, it would not have been ethical for Clinton to continue to hedge on the U.S.-Mexico Free Trade Agreement or for President Bush to refuse to specify where he would cut programs to reduce the deficit. Candidates should not withhold information that matters to voters. The ethics of democratic choice demand more than the late Senator Tom Connally's response when he was challenged by a voter to say where he stood on price supports for cotton. "I'm all right on that," Connally snapped as he hurried for the door.

A hedge is ethical when a candidate makes it clear that her mind is not made up completely, when she is conflicted about what to do, or when she gives an indication of her thinking but frankly says that she wants to keep her options open because the issue is so complicated. It is not only foolish but unethical to say you will never raise taxes or go to war. When confronted with a complicated issue such as how to provide for comprehensive health care, it is ethical to specify the system you currently prefer but to stop short of saying that you will approve that system alone and no others. On a politically complex problem like the deficit, promising to bring it under control by a certain date is foolhardy and unethical. A hedge on a specific time for fixing the deficit is probably more ethical than a firm promise. In a democracy, it is likely that some compromise will be necessary to achieve any result. It is unethical to harden a position so that reasonable political alternatives cannot be considered. To do so is to apply to the polity Sayre's law of the academy, which holds that academic controversies are so bitter because the stakes are so low and because the people of honor are always outnumbered by the people of principle.

Given a choice, many candidates would rather not get too specific about what they will do about certain problems once elected. Most know, or at least suspect, that once in office they will find that many of the problems that look simple from the perspective of a challenger will turn out to be wicked and complex. We also know, almost instinctively, that the great issues of a campaign often turn out to be eclipsed by other, more urgent matters, necessitating their neglect once the winner is in office. Thus, some vagueness in prescription seems ethically tolerable. Certainly it is preferable to an unequivocal pledge that is almost universally recognized as unlikely to be kept. The problem, then, is how vague a campaign promise can be without colliding with the obligation of a candidate to reveal enough to give voters an informed choice.

F. Lies

> "Here lies a politician and an honest man," the tombstone read.
> "Too bad they had to bury two people in the same grave," says the cynic.

Since Machiavelli's *The Prince*, there has been a presumption that politicians would lie to advance their own interests as well as the interests of the state. Like other humans who want something badly, politicians are tempted to lie, if necessary, to achieve it. Campaign communications contain almost all the basic classifications of lies.

Campaigns are often festivals of white lies—defined as lies that are excused as harmless, but if believed can be not only misleading but corrosive to the believer, the liar, and the system. The most common white lies are those associated with the campaign biography, which, as we have already seen, sometimes improves on the truth.

No one expects candidates to speak ill of themselves. An absence of puffery would, however, serve two important purposes. Because one of the clues voters seek in assessing candidates is to understand what has formed their views of the world and how they have behaved in coping with what life has dealt them, a balanced understanding of a candidate's history is important. To the extent that campaign puffery obscures that candid assessment, it diminishes the public's capacity to choose.

Second, campaign biographies that exaggerate a candidate's accomplishments and leadership qualities mislead the public and set it up for disillusionment when their hero of November is discovered by midterm to have feet of clay starting just below the armpits. It would probably be far better for democracy for us to realize that our politicians are much like other leaders of large organizations—reasonably talented and reasonably flawed human beings.

One of the most common forms of lying in campaign communications is misrepresentation of an opponent's record or positions on an issue. Candidates misrepresent their opponents because it is often easier to criticize or refute the distorted view than the real one. A misrepresentation can force a candidate onto the defensive, spending valuable time clarifying a position or recovering from fear spread by the opposition. In the recent campaign, Clinton's record on taxes was repeatedly misrepresented by the Bush campaign. Challenged by the press, a campaign official acknowledged the lie but said it would continue to be used because "it works."

Leviticus, Chapter 20, tells of the ceremony in which the sins of the people were placed upon the head of a scapegoat, which was then driven into the wilderness. In politics, this ritual purification is carried out by identifying a person or group that can be blamed for follies or mistakes of policy and driving them—and incidentally the politicians who allegedly have sustained or tolerated "them"—into the political wilderness.

A venerable scapegoat in American political campaigns has been racial and national minorities. Until the civil rights revolution, blacks were often blamed openly for white economic problems. In modern campaigns, racial scapegoats are still used, but the language is coded. The 1990 campaign commercial by Senator Jesse Helms showing white hands crumpling a job rejection notice and blaming it on affirmative action programs supported by the Senator's black opponent illustrates the lasting effectiveness of racial scapegoating.

A straw man is a fiction concocted to divert attention from the actual problems confronted by the electorate. By attacking the straw, the candidate fakes courage and assumes a posture of the champion against the evil attributed to his opponent. "Gutting Social Security" has for years been the favorite straw man of Democratic candidates.

The 1992 entry in the straw man (or woman) sweepstakes was the "cultural elite," which Vice President Quayle blamed for the decline in family values, symbolized by the TV sitcom *Murphy Brown*. The attraction of a straw such as the cultural elite is that almost no one will own up to being it, especially when it is defined as "those who" scorn values that are in widespread favor. The straw allows the audience to identify itself as the endangered "we." It places the political opponent in the uncomfortable position of having to second the concern, to claim as much patriotism or virtue as the first to attack the straw, and to sound thereby as if she comes only lately and reluctantly to the cause. The problem with making a straw of a popular television program, however, was that it could, and did, strike back. A really good straw cannot speak for itself.

An advantage of the straw issue is that it usually has nothing to do with actual performance of the office. Thus, the famous Willie Horton ad in 1988 and the attack on trial lawyers in 1992 did not address issues that the next President would have to deal with in any significant way.

Attacks on scapegoats and straws appeal to emotion rather than reason. They are often cheap shots at groups or institutions that cannot defend themselves—sometimes because they do not really exist in the form in which they are attacked. The attacks manufacture a campaign issue that may have little to do with governing. Moreover, they divert attention from serious public problems the candidate should be held accountable for discussing to a pseudo issue that has no relevance past election day.

Comedian George Burns once said, "Sincerity is the secret to success. When you can fake that, you've got it made." Scapegoating and attacking a straw are consistently among the most successful ways of faking one's sincerity without risking the prospect of subsequent accountability for some actual decision.

Scapegoating and the use of straw issues are unethical per se. I can think of no publicly defensible moral justification for either. They do not inform the public. They do not force debate on serious issues. They are propaganda devices designed to divert attention from such debate. That they are clever is certain. Ethics can tolerate cleverness, but it requires more. There are always alternatives, the chief one of which is to address real problems.

Leadership

In a democracy, campaigns are the closest we get to a protracted dialogue between the people and their leaders. James McGregor Burns has argued that leadership is primarily about ethics rather than power. Campaign communications establish the ethical foundations on which official leadership is then built. To be sure, campaigns are about winning. But they are also about mandates and accountability. A cynical and manipulative campaign may produce an electoral victory, but the knowledge that they have been manipulated undermines the people's acceptance of the legitimacy of the resulting government. Victory can be made hollow by corroding the trust that binds leaders and followers. Two examples from this past campaign year illustrate how campaign communications can affect the ethics of leadership.

First, let us look at the two campaigns of Ross Perot. Here was a candidacy that promised an ethical campaign for an ethical objective. Perot promised to tell us the truth; to do what had to be done to save the nation from economic disaster; to pull no punches, take no shortcuts, bite no sounds, doctor no spins, and level with the American people.

Perot hit a central nerve in the American political system. He appealed deeply to many citizens who view politics as inherently a dirty business populated by charlatans and to others who had felt their trust betrayed too often by the usual crowd of dedicated office seekers. These civic purists saw in Perot someone who could cleanse the system, a modern Cromwell playing Mr. Smith Goes to Washington.

In July, when Perot withdrew from the race, he provided no core around which his supporters could rally to sustain their movement. His actions reduced the Perot bubble to a cult of the personality, which could not exist without him. Even though he continued to protest, "This is not about me," unfortunately, it was. He seemed to apply business ethics to politics, to look upon his candidacy as a business proposition. Once the investment of his time looked like it might turn sour, he cut his losses and bailed out. In business, this is a perfectly ethical decision. It conserves scarce resources and fosters more efficient businesses.

In politics, however, such behavior is less than admirable, for it ignores a leader's responsibility to his followers to respect them, to recognize that the leader is obligated to the followers rather than the other way around. Leadership is earned by serving the interests of followers and by making an ethical argument for their support. This obligation is that much greater when a leader invokes moral reasons, as Perot did, for his candidacy.

Having enticed people to support him in a cause justified on moral grounds, Perot had an ethical obligation to justify his withdrawal to the movement he had created in a way that could be accepted as morally understandable, if regrettable. Instead, he essentially said that he did not think he could win, so to hell with it. What Perot seems not to have understood until later was that, although his supporters surely wanted to win, they wanted even more to have a means of mobilizing their concern for their country and a cause in which they could exercise their voice in the political system in preference to exiting it. Instead, he showed them the door, increasing the cynicism his candidacy had initially done much to quash.

Perot's reentry into presidential politics in October can only be described as manipulative. Having subsidized his book onto the best-seller list and his name onto the ballot in every state, Perot began to hint that he might reenter the race if his "volunteers" demanded it. His state coordinators drummed up support, and his 800 number recorded all calls as supporting reentry.

Perot now had a program as well as an indictment of existing policy, but he disdained the same standards of accountability expected of other candidates. Except for the debates and a few public speeches to supporters, he ran a reclusive campaign through infomercials and spot advertising on radio and television. His press conferences degenerated into attacks on the media as soon as reporters raised questions he preferred not to answer. While his television appearances were commendable for their attention to substantive policy issues, Perot basically refused to subject his proposals to the scrutiny of public and media discourse. His insistence on financing his own campaign, spending more on advertising in the last two weeks than both national party candidates combined, was touted as evidence of his independence. It also was a symbol of his unaccountability to anyone, including his own supporters. While he continued to insist that "I belong to you!" he marched only to his own tune.

The second illustration of how campaign communications illuminate the ethics of leadership can be found in a small incident in the Clinton campaign—the Sister Souljah controversy. Following the Los Angeles riots, Souljah, a rap singer, told the *Washington Post* that some black youths felt that if blacks were spending so much time killing blacks, maybe there ought to be a week in which they killed whites. Clinton used his speech to Jesse Jackson's Rainbow Coalition to decry these remarks as not dissimilar from what one might expect to hear, on the other side of the racial divide, from David Duke. Jackson took harsh exception to Clinton's criticism, defending the rapper as being quoted out of context and likening Clinton's remarks to the "race card" played in 1988 by the Willie Horton commercial. Sister Souljah herself then attacked Clinton as a hypocrite.

Several ethical issues are involved in this event, involving its motivation, content, timing, and venue. As a campaign communication, the comments by Clinton were strategically important. They were calculated to convey the image of a candidate who was committed to racial harmony but willing to risk the enmity of a powerful figure, Jackson, in order to demonstrate that the candidate would not subordinate the moral issue of even-handedness in racial matters to pandering for popularity with Jackson and his more radical constituency.

Notwithstanding Clinton's commitment and record of work to improve interracial understanding, Jackson and others argued that the candidate's motive was not understanding but campaign positioning—showing that he could "stand up" to Jackson and, symbolically, to all special interests, thus defusing one of the central attacks made on Democratic presidential hopefuls for the past generation. It does not follow, however, that a candidate should eschew saying something he believes is right because it might advance his stature.

If Clinton honestly believed that it was important to admonish those who express racial hatred and that a President has a duty to set a moral example in such matters, the fact that making the statement may have benefited his campaign is incidental. There was some evidence, of course, that the statement could damage his campaign. Jackson's enmity could have spelled trouble among black voters, who are a key to the success of any Democratic candidate. Thus it was not clear, on balance, whether the statement would actually help or hurt the candidacy. This analysis supports the idea that the motivation for the communication was not ethically suspect.

The content of the statement is above ethical criticism. It condemned appeals to racial violence. But was Clinton using the statement and the occasion to appeal to white racism in the name of denouncing black racism? An ethical analysis requires us to recognize that the words themselves cannot be considered in isolation but must be looked at in the context of the total speech, the history of the speaker, and the event. Clinton's speech dealt with the problems of racial sensitivity. He used his own recent faux pas of playing golf at a segregated country club as an illustration of how people can be insensitive to the feelings of others. He noted that he had talked about race relations to white groups and that he had made improvement of race relations a centerpiece of his campaign. In this context, the remarks about Sister Souljah's harsh statement would have been ethically unexceptional at another place or time.

But what about the place and time? As far as place was concerned, moral arguments carry the greatest force when made at a place that contributes to their impact. Had Martin Luther posted the 95 Theses on the door of the post office, they would not have had quite the impact they had at the cathedral. Certainly the place was not unethically chosen. Does it matter that it made the hosts uncomfortable? I think not. The hosts were a person and an organization also committed to racial justice and harmony. By choosing the Rainbow Coalition as his venue, Clinton gave a greater ring of authenticity to his criticism than if it had been made at a suburban rally.

If Clinton is subject to ethical criticism at all, it would be on his timing. Sister Souljah's statement was made a month before the Rainbow Coalition meeting, although she did speak to the Coalition the day before Clinton. At that time, however, she did not make any especially provocative remarks. Therefore, Clinton's rebuke, by not being timely, may have lost some of its moral authority and authenticity.

On balance, whatever the actual consequences of this particular campaign communication, it is hard to argue

that it was unethical. Every campaign communication
should be designed to appeal to some constituency. This
one had some appeal across racial lines, as evidenced by
the number of black leaders who endorsed Clinton's comment. Did it also appeal to some whites? Surely it did.
Candidates cannot be expected to say only those things
that will harm their prospects for election. That is an
ethical standard too severe for humans to meet.

Woodrow Wilson once said that a leader must take the
moral high ground. In his remarks to the Rainbow Coalition, Clinton followed Wilson's advice. Even though he
surely offended his hosts, who were at least putative
followers, they could not criticize the substance of what
he said, only its venue and timing. But these remarks
also got across the idea that Clinton understood a leader's
ethical obligation to deal authentically and forthrightly
with supporters from his own experience and values,
even at the risk of offending some of them some of the
time.

Conclusion

"The public, I suspect, is an ass," H. L. Mencken once
wrote. Campaign consultants often appear to share
Mencken's suspicion that you bcan almost never under-
estimate the intelligence of the American voter. As an
ethical principle, this is not very elevating. One can
accept the last part of Lincoln's adage that "you can't fool
all of the people all of the time" as a cautionary note while
recognizing the phrase, "You can fool all of the people
some of the time" as the watchword of a campaign. The
problem with fooling people is that doing so has serious
consequences for democratic governance.

Dozens of books and articles deplore the state of campaign communications, but few discuss the ethics of

campaigning. Thousands of pages, however, describe the techniques of crafting campaign propaganda. The "boys will be boys" approach to the ethics of campaigning has become so pervasive that we now are treated to learned and admiring discussions during the course of the campaign about the techniques of opinion manipulation used on us by each camp. Candidates, instead of being criticized for unleashing a particularly nasty and distorted attack on an opponent, are admired for the cleverness of it. The hapless victim is likely to be criticized for not responding in kind. That "everybody does it" is not a justification for unethical campaigning. Instead, it is reason for alarm and for demanding that this long and dishonorable tradition be brought to an end.

Although campaigns reverberate with the metaphors of war, they are not military engagements. Nor are they sporting events. Surely no one can believe that democracy will be made better if candidates improve their skills at either war or liars' poker. No change will come about, however, if no one demands it and if no candidate who engages in deceptive or manipulative campaigning pays the price for being good at being bad. There are some encouraging signs, even in Texas. The defeat of Lena Guerrero for election to the Texas Railroad Commission seems directly attributable to the falsification of her academic credentials. The insistence of citizen panelists in the second presidential debate that the candidates address issues rather than engage in ad hominem attacks was also an encouraging sign that public patience with such tactics is wearing thin. On the other hand, the evidence from the opinion polls showed that negative campaigning, however untrue, substantially affected attitudes toward candidates.

Given the challenge and the temptations before them,

we cannot depend upon the opposing parties and candidates to serve as ethical watchdogs of campaign communications. They will, however, bend to persistent public demands for more ethical conduct, but only if such demands are backed by the defeat of those who engage in unethical campaigning.

The press can serve us better by specifically pointing out ethical lapses. They began to do this after the 1988 campaign through analyses of campaign commercials. That was a helpful start, but more is needed, in the way of regular analytical reports on the content of ads, speeches, and other communications from and on behalf of candidates. Many newspapers have added ombudsmen who comment regularly on the ethics of news coverage. An ethicist in residence during political campaigns could be helpful, as an independent critic of all candidates, applying the same, clearly stated ethical standards to all campaign communications and tactics. The occasional appearance of ethicists, instead of partisan spin doctors, on political talk shows would be a welcome relief.

Public interest watchdog organizations, such as the old Fair Campaign Practices Commissions, could also play a significant role. The presence of a nonpartisan or bipartisan group of whistle-blowers might discourage candidates from indulging in ethically questionable communications if they then could expect to spend valuable campaign time defending themselves. Roger Ailes, the architect of the 1968 Nixon communications strategy and the 1988 Bush attack ads, is said to be a stickler for documentation, but only to the extent that there must be at least a shred of evidence in support of any allegation. That is a standard that is shredding public confidence in the electoral process. It is inconceivable that, if a public discussion of campaigning were held before each election, people would consent in advance to being lied to, to having critical information withheld from them, to being told only those things they wanted to hear, or to being gulled by advertisements supported by only the smallest bit of evidence or an unsuported allegation.

I doubt that we can legislate public ethics. States that have tried to criminalize unethical campaign practices tend to produce silly excesses of prosecutorial zeal. Indicting candidates for misstating an opponent's campaign literature, falsely claiming an endorsement, or serving Twinkies to senior citizens (in violation of a law forbidding offering anything of value to a voter) can itself be unethically used to partisan advantage. Rather than try to codify campaign ethics, we need to expose publicly those campaigns and candidates who fail to meet even the low standards they set for themselves. We must, in short, raise the cost of sleaze.

Sissela Bok has stated the case well:

> "Whenever lies to the public have become routine, then very special safeguards should be required. The test of public justification of deceptive practices is more needed than ever.... Those in government and other positions of trust should be held to the highest standards. Their lies are not ennobled by their positions; quite the contrary. . . . [O]nly those deceptive practices which can be openly debated and consented to in advance are *justifiable* in a democracy." (*Lying*, p. 181.)

An argument has often been made that a different ethical standard should apply to politicians, given the hazards of the occupation. Officials, we are reminded, may be obliged to lie in the interests of the state. Indeed, the task of the politician is complex. He must find the resonant chords of popular opinion before he can lead. That task involves trial and error—trying out notes, muting them when necessary, and even changing tunes. This is not just a matter of preference for ambiguity, but a necessity in building a coalition capable of legitimately governing a pluralistic society. Hubert Humphrey once told a group of my students that "of course" he compromised his principles. If you are going to get anything done in a democracy, he said, you have to compromise because the other fellow is not interested in compromising with you on something you care nothing about. He might well have added one of his favorite aphorisms about taking responsibility for one's actions: "To err is human. To blame someone else is politics."

All of this suggests that we as citizens have to be willing to cut our politicians a little slack. In order to have a pretty good idea of what they will try to accomplish, we need not nail them down to unequivocal promises to never, never, never change their minds. We should, indeed, be deeply suspicious of the politician who makes such promises. At the same time, we have the right to insist that whether a politician hews to the line on a campaign promise or executes a seamless reversal of position, we are entitled to an explanation that can pass the laugh test.

Democracy is not an easy system to maintain. It is much more than an exercise in the stacking of meetings. Politics, as Aristotle recognized, is fundamentally an exercise in ethics. Its practice in a democracy requires that the public, as well as its leaders, remain ever ethically alert.

CENSORSHIP: HISTORICAL BACKGROUND AND JUSTIFIABLE FORMS

by

Andrew R. Cecil

Andrew R. Cecil

Andrew R. Cecil is Distinguished Scholar in Residence at The University of Texas at Dallas. In February 1979 the University established in his honor the Andrew R. Cecil Lectures on Moral Values in a Free Society and invited Dr. Cecil to deliver the first series of lectures in November 1979. The first annual proceedings were published as Dr. Cecil's book The Third Way: Enlightened Capitalism and the Search for a New Social Order, *which received an enthusiastic response. He has also lectured in each subsequent series. A new book,* The Foundations of a Free Society, *was published in 1983.* Three Sources of National Strength *appeared in 1986, and* Equality, Tolerance, and Loyalty *in 1990. In 1976 the University named for Dr. Cecil the Andrew R. Cecil Auditorium, and in 1990 it established the Andrew R. Cecil Endowed Chair in Applied Ethics.*

Educated in Europe and well launched on a career as a professor and practitioner in the fields of law and economics, Dr. Cecil resumed his academic career after World War II in Lima, Peru, at the University of San Marcos. After 1949, he was associated with the Methodist church-affiliated colleges and universities in the United States until he joined The Southwestern Legal Foundation. Associated with the Foundation since 1958, Dr. Cecil helped guide its development of five educational centers that offer nationally and internationally recognized programs in advanced continuing education. Since his retirement as President of the Foundation, he serves as Chancellor Emeritus and Honorary Trustee.

Dr. Cecil is author of fifteen books on the subjects of law, economics, and religion and of more than seventy articles on these subjects and on the philosophy of religion published in periodicals and anthologies. A member of the American Society of International Law, of the American Branch of the International Law Association, and of the American Judicature Society, Dr. Cecil has served on numerous commissions for the Methodist Church and is a member of the Board of Trustees of the National Methodist Foundation for Christian Higher Education. In 1981 he was named an Honorary Rotarian.

CENSORSHIP: HISTORICAL BACKGROUND AND JUSTIFIABLE FORMS

by

Andrew R. Cecil

Censorship can be defined as the official government suppression of any public expression that a governing authority believes to threaten either its power or the accepted social and moral order. Throughout history, censorship has earned a negative set of associations. It has primarily been identified as a tool for suppressing the exchange of ideas, exercised by authorities desiring to protect their entrenched interests.

The purpose of my lecture is twofold. First, I wish to provide an historical overview of censorship. Second, since other lecturers in the series will undoubtedly refer to the harmful effects of censorship, I shall undertake the task of pointing out the kinds of censorship that may have a constructive effect in preserving national security and in maintaining the orderly administration of justice.

Historical Overview

Censorship has appeared at all stages of history, in almost all parts of the world. The most common cause has been to consolidate the power of a ruler or ruling class. In ancient China, for instance, Shih huang-ti, the "first universal emperor," who built the Great Wall, ordered in 213 B.C. the destruction of the existing classics of the national literature in order to combat the Chinese literati, who had criticized his reign. Thousands of scholars were banished and hundreds executed.

Among the burned books was the *Analects* of Confucius, who with his followers had advocated a free exchange of ideas as the best manner of achieving and promoting wisdom. Such an attitude, however, was felt to be in opposition to the absolute governmental power that the new emperor was seeking.

In the Old Testament, the prophet could speak out against the king or his actions with relative impunity. When Nathan rebuked David for his sin of adultery, David repented. The role of the prophets and their freedom of expression were respected as a part of Hebrew tradition.

Such freedom, however, did not apply to expressions that might offend the governing authority of God. In this theocratic society, blasphemy was the ultimate sin and thus the ultimate crime. We find in the Ten Commandments that the name of the Lord is to be accorded the same respect as the Lord Himself. The Decalogue, because of a fear of idolatry, also severely limits activities that we might regard as artistic expression.

> "Thou shalt not make unto thee any graven image, or any likeness of anything that is in heaven above, or that is in the earth beneath, or that is in the water under earth: Thou shalt not bow down thyself to them, nor serve them." (Exodus 20:4–5.)

A. Ancient Greece and Rome

Ancient Greece has long been seen as the birthplace of freedom. The great English poet John Milton in his masterly defense of free speech and publication, the *Areopagitica* (which we shall examine in more detail later), claimed that in Athens the authorities allowed freedom of all sorts of writing except two—blasphemy (or atheism) and libel. In fact, Milton drew the title of his tract arguing for liberty in publication from the Areopagus, the meeting place of the high court of Athens, which he held up as an ideal.

Even in Athens, however, the freedom of speech and ideas had some limitations, motivated primarily by political considerations. The youth of the city enlisted under the banner of the teachings of the philosopher Socrates, who believed that God commanded him to persuade others not to care for body or money in place of, or as much as, excellence of soul. Socrates remained loyal to the laws of the state, even if they were unjust. When Athens—misgoverned because of an individualism that disintegrated the social fabric, beaten and humiliated in the ill-fated Peloponnesian wars—sought a scapegoat for its demoralization, it condemned Socrates for corrupting the morals of the young, for scorning democracy with his aristocratic gospel, and for endangering the welfare of the state by his teaching. The charge against him was impiety, but the real reason for his persecution was political.

With the collapse of the Athenians' virtues, under the rule of the passion-ridden "direct democracy" in which a crowd of thousands of citizens made every decision, Socrates was sacrificed to the bigotry of the fallen city and the censorship of the angry, passion-led mob. He was convicted and condemned to drink the poison hemlock. His choice was to die as "a victim of injustice at the hands of men" rather than to escape and trespass the law and "thus shamefully return injustice for injustice and injury for injury." (*Crito* 54c, in *The Dialogues of Plato*, Vol. I, trans. by R.E. Allen, Yale University Press, 1984, p. 129.)

Socrates' teaching was immortalized by Plato, an admiring student who praised God that he was "born in the age of Socrates." Plato's quest for absolute and eternal values was combined with his concern for the world in which he lived. For the sake of preserving his concept of an ideal republic and of introducing the minds of the youth to the high aspirations of that republic, he established the principle of a moral censorship of literature and of all other forms of art. Plato justified such censorship because of the impact literature and the arts could have on the formation of the character of the individual and on the well-being of society in general.

Long before Plato, the Greek philosophers Heraclitus and Xenophanes disapproved of Homer's immoral stories about the gods. Notwithstanding all Plato's admiration for Homer and Hesiod, he advocated the censorship of those writers in order to reject their fictions, which he termed "suicidal, ruinous, impious," for young persons who cannot judge what is allegorical and what is literal. Mothers and nurses, he argued, should therefore be allowed to tell their children only stories authorized by the censors. Plato saw the fault of the poets in their descriptions of the crimes committed by the gods, of their quarrels among themselves, of their plots and fights against one another. The long list of Plato's accusations against Homer point to his "guilt of the folly" of describing the gods as the dispensers of both good and evil. According to Plato, God and the things of God are in every way perfect; therefore, "let this then be one of our rules and principles concerning the gods to which our poets and reciters will be expected to conform—that God is not the author of all things, but of good only." (*The Republic and Other Works*, trans. by B. Jowett, Anchor Books, 1973, pp. 62–66.)

Plato recommended censorship not only of writers but also of practitioners of other arts, such as musicians, painters, and architects. To prevent the corruption of the souls of the Guardians—who represent the supreme authority of government in Plato's ideal republic—and their growing up "amid images of moral deformity," Plato in *The Republic* asked artists and writers to express only the image of the good in their works:

> "Let our artists rather be those who are gifted to discern the true nature of the beautiful and the graceful; then will our youth dwell in a land of health, amid fair sights and sounds, and receive the good in everything; and beauty, the effluence of fair works, shall flow into the eye and ear, like a health-giving breeze from a purer region, and sensibly draw the soul from earliest years into likeness and sympathy with the beauty of reason." (*Id.*, p. 90.)

Both Plato and Aristotle, his successor, sought to relate art to morality as well as to the benefits it provides to mankind. Aristotle pointed out that

> "to be learning something is the greatest of pleasures not only to the philosopher but also to the rest of mankind, however small their capacity for it; the reason of the delight in seeing the picture is that one is at the same time learning—gathering the meaning of things." (*Nichomachean Ethics*, trans. by Martin Oswald, The Library of Liberal Arts, 1962, p. 1457.)

It was the Roman statesman and philosopher Cicero who, following his studies in Greece, brought the treasures of Greek thought within the reach of the Roman public. Cicero, the great master of Latin prose whose orations and private letters won him a prominent place in the history of literature and of the search for both human rights and moral rectitude, was proscribed and killed in 43 B.C., a year after the murder of Julius Caesar. (After Caesar's assassination, Cicero had tried to become the leader of a revived republicanism, which caused Mark Antony to put Cicero's name among the proscriptions.) Cicero's writings reveal the high ideals of the Roman republic and give a taste of political life during the period. Their importance as a moral influence has never waned.

It may be noted that in ancient Rome the office of the censor, established in 443 B.C., was responsible not only for taking the census of the inhabitants of Rome but also for protecting Rome from immorality. The latter function included protecting the government from criticism. In order to "curb immorality," there were occasions when philosophers, statesmen, actors, and poets were banished and the Senate was purged by executive order.

Roman law served as a model legal system, largely because it provided a bulwark of law and justice for its citizens. Except for its survival in some aspects of the canon law of the medieval church, Roman law was largely forgotten after the fall of the empire. The peoples who grew into the modern western European nations evolved their legal systems out of tribal, and later feudal, law. With the Renaissance's renewed interest in Greek and Roman culture, Roman law once again was used as the basis for the legal systems of many nations of the world.

B. Church Censorship

In the Middle Ages, the Catholic Church aspired to become the successor of the Roman empire. The popes tried to assert their omnipotence as lawmakers and supreme judges. In this era of feudalism and scholasticism, the church ruled over vast estates that belonged to it in perpetuity, and the intellectual life of the time centered in the clergy. This vast concentration of power—religious, political, and intellectual—was reinforced by an overwhelming pressure toward conformity. Censorship aimed at heretics who dissented from this prevailing conformity was marked by the wholesale and ferocious slaughter of tens of thousands of victims. The "Christian" inquisitors used torture and extreme cruelty to obtain confessions, and those who were unrepentant were burned alive.

Ironically, the Inquisition was at first intended as a merciful way of dealing with doctrinal deviance. As Milton pointed out in the *Areopagitica*, for many centuries the church was neither deeply engaged nor cruel in combatting dissent. But in southern Europe during the Middle Ages (beginning in the eleventh century), the rise of Catharism—the unorthodox pursuit of perfection also known as Albigensianism—posed a new problem for church authorities. In many cities and villages, the common people were taking doctrinal disputes into their own hands and murdering their neighbors. The Inquisition was established by Pope Gregory IX in 1242 partly to combat such lynch psychology, and many of the earlier inquisitors genuinely sought justice and even mercy for the unorthodox. (See Bernard Hamilton, *The Medieval Inquisition*, Holmes & Meier Publishers Inc., 1981.) It was only when the Inquisition became institutionalized in later years that the horrifying abuses known to history came to predominate.

With the invention of the printing press, the publication of, rather than the mere belief in, dissenting ideas became the main focus of church censorship. The thirteenth century, when the Inquisition was set up, was also a period of the rise of the universities. Largely clerical, they centered on the dialectics of theology. As censorship expanded, the universities helped the church in performing the function of judging books by supplying experts to serve as members of boards of censors. The right of the church to censor was asserted by the Fifth Lateran Council (1512–1517), which was convened by Pope Julius II and continued by Leo X, and which forbade the printing of books without ecclesiastical authorization.

Although since ancient times books had frequently been condemned by the church, it was Pope Paul IV, the chief organizer of the Holy Roman Inquisition, who in 1559 introduced the word "Index" in the title of a list of forbidden books *(Index Librorum Prohibitorum)*. The Council of Trent in the third period of its sessions (1562–1563) discussed such a listing of forbidden books and established ten general rules for the control of books already condemned by the church. It also called for the examination and licensing of books before their publication. The Index thus established continued to be official church policy until Pope Leo XIII reformed it in 1900, and it survived in a somewhat changed form until well into the age of Vatican II.

The censorship and the intolerance applied by the church in the era since the Middle Ages were abominable. In my essay on "Tolerance" (Cecil, *Equality, Tolerance, and Loyalty,* The University of Texas at Dallas, 1990, pp. 105–153), I listed some of the cruelties experienced by those who dared to dissent with the church. They were executed—burned to death or hanged or subjected to yet worse torture. The extent of such censorship is illustrated by the condemnation of John Wycliffe, whose translation of the Bible was an important landmark in the history of English literature, for spreading the doctrine that the Scriptures are the supreme authority of the faith. He was twice condemned, and the pope ordered his books to be burned.

By a decree of the Council of Constance (1415), Wycliffe's remains were dug up from his grave and burned. This desecration was carried out at the command of Pope Martin V. Jan Huss, the Bohemian reformer and the leading opponent of the condemnation of Wycliffe's writings, presented himself at the Council of Constance under the protection of Emperor Sigismund's safe-conduct, only to be imprisoned, tried, and burned at the stake as a heretic.

Such persecution extended even to matters that were mainly scientific and not religious. When Galileo in 1632 confirmed the acceptance of the Copernican theory of the solar system, denounced by the church as dangerous to the faith, he was tried by the Inquisition and obliged to adjust the "error" in his belief that the sun is the central body and the earth with the other planets revolves around it. His indefinite imprisonment was ended only by Pope Urban VIII. (*Id.*, pp. 114–116.)

Church censorship was not limited to ecclesiastical authorities who maintained allegiance to Rome. After the Reformation, the early Protestants, like the Catholics, believed that any opposition to their religious practices implied evil and had to be eradicated. Hugo Grotius, the Dutch humanist and jurist, was sentenced to life imprisonment and forfeiture of all property for endorsing the Arminian faction in its controversy with the Gomarist faction of the Protestants in the Netherlands. The Arminians challenged the doctrine of unconditional predestination, a challenge that contradicted the conservative Calvinism that was strong in the Netherlands. After his conviction in 1619 for treason and imprisonment, Grotius escaped into France, where hé published his famous masterpiece, *De Jure Belli ac Pacis.*

When the Protestant Reformation began with Martin Luther's Ninety-five Theses (October 31, 1517), Pope Leo X in the bull *Exsurge Domine* condemned him and excommunicated the Reformers. In response Luther burned the bull, along with a copy of the canon law. After his appearance at the Diet of Worms, where he refused to change his position (April 1521), Luther's friends, in order to save his life, placed him in the Castle of Wartburg in Thuringia, where he produced his German translation of the New Testament, published in 1522. The unauthorized translations of Scripture and the works of Luther and Calvin were included among the books condemned under the rules of the abovementioned Council of Trent.

C. *The Struggle for Freedom of the Press*

As suggested above, it was the introduction of printing in France (1470) and England (1476) that brought about profound changes in methods of censorship. Prepublication censorship gained in importance and was exercised not only by ecclesiastical bodies but also by secular governmental officials. The French Parliament, for instance, ordered Voltaire's book *Letters on the English* to be publicly burned since it contrasted English political liberty with French tyranny. The French scholar Nicolas Fréret (1688–1749) was sent to jail for advancing the theory that the French were in origin a Germanic people and not of Greco-Latin descent and for questioning the origins of royal power in France. The French encyclopedist and philosopher Denis Diderot (1713-1784) was jailed for his *Letter on the Blind*. Books continued to be burned in France even after the fall of Napoleon, when the Bourbons were restored to the French throne.

Each action causes a reaction. The growth of censorship was met with a rising voice crying out for freedom of the press and of speech. The intellectual ferment of the seventeenth and eighteenth centuries was permeated by the idea that no laws should stifle the growth of freedom, including freedom of speech and freedom of the press.

1. Milton

We have already mentioned the great English poet John Milton (1608-1674), who was one of the earliest and most eloquent defenders of freedom of publication. Milton became embroiled in the controversy over freedom of the press when—following his separation from Mary Powell, who left him a month after their marriage—he wrote a series of pamphlets arguing the morality of divorce for incompatibility of temperament. In violation of existing laws, the pamphlets were printed without obtaining a prepublication license. When accused of violating the law, Milton wrote the *Areopagitica*, in which he surveyed the history of censorship and reasoned that prepublication licensing of printed material was an unwarranted intrusion on God-given liberty.

Milton's attack on censorship is the most eloquent ever written. He is especially passionate about the power of the printed word:

> "For books are not absolutely dead things, but do contain a potency of life in them to be as active as that soul was whose progeny they are; nay they do preserve as in a vial the purest efficacy and extrac-

tion of that living intellect that bred them. . . . [A]s good almost kill a man as kill a good book; who kills a man kills a reasonable creature, God's image; but he who destroys a good book kills reason itself, kills the image of God, as it were in the eye. Many a man lives a burden to the earth; but a good book is the precious lifeblood of a master spirit, embalmed and treasured up on purpose to a life beyond life." (*The Prose of John Milton*, ed. by J. Max Patrick, New York University Press, 1968, pp. 271–272.)

Milton argued that the Pauline epistles encourage Christians to test all things, not to avoid encountering them. Indeed, the poet remonstrates, scripture itself recounts episodes of sin and blasphemy, even arguments against providence that are not unlike those of the skeptical pagan philosopher Epicurus. The ancient church fathers, such as Clement and Eusebius, recounted lewd pagan rites in order to dissuade Christians from participating in them. Milton's primary argument is that true Christian faith and morals are not so weak that they cannot stand up to error or temptation:

"He that can apprehend and consider vice with all her baits and seeming pleasures, and yet abstain, and yet distinguish, and yet prefer that which is truly better, he is the true warfaring Christian. I cannot praise a fugitive and cloistered virtue, unexercised and unbreathed, that never sallies out and sees her adversary, but slinks out of the race, where that immortal garland is to be run for, not without dust and heat." (*Id.*, pp. 287–288.)

For Milton, not all books were good; some authors, he believed, should be punished for their publications in certain circumstances. In the Greek liberty of thought that he held up as his initial ideal in the *Areopagitica*, he noted that the authorities punished only writings that were "either blasphemous and atheistical, or libelous." Milton also praised the Parliamentarians he was addressing for ordering that all printed books include the name of author and publisher, so that those found to be "mischievous and libelous" could be punished.

The great poet declined to define precisely the limits of what he considered mischievous—probably this included books dangerous to law and order, superstitious, or impious—but there is no doubt that, despite his insistence that freedom of the press was essential to the pursuit of truth, he believed that some publications should be legally prosecuted. But he utterly opposed the practice of requiring any books to be licensed before publication by a governmental censor. (In recent controversies in our own country, this process was called prior judicial restraint.)

More than two decades after the publication of the *Areopagitica* in 1644, Milton found himself the victim of censorship. He had been a part of the Puritan government of Oliver Cromwell that had ruled England after the revolution against King Charles I. At the Restoration (the reestablishment of monarchical government on the accession of Charles II), Milton was forced into hiding for having published *The Readie Easy Way to Establish a Free Commonwealth*, and some of his books were burned. Only when a general amnesty was granted was he able to return to complete his greatest works, which placed him in the ranks of the most illustrious English poets.

2. Spinoza

Among the prominent philosophers who advocated

freedom of speech and the press we should list Baruch Spinoza, John Locke, and John Stuart Mill. Spinoza (1632–1677), whose book *Treatise on Religion and the State* (*Tractatus Theologico-Politicus*) "graced" the Index Librorum Prohibitorum, saw real liberty as the goal of government. "The last end of the state," he wrote, "is not to dominate men, not to restrain them by fear; rather it is so to free each man from fear that he may live and act with full security and without injury to himself or his neighbor."

Spinoza held in abhorrence the laws against free discussion and free speech that existed in his time:

> "It is far from possible to impose uniformity of speech, for the more rulers strive to curtail freedom of speech, the more obstinately are they resisted. . . . Men, as generally constituted, are most prone to resent the branding as criminal of opinions which they believe to be true . . . ; hence they are ready to forswear the laws and conspire against the authorities, thinking it not shameful but honorable to stir up seditions and perpetrate any sort of crime with this end in view. Such being the constitution of human nature, we see that laws directed against opinions affect the generous-minded rather than the wicked, and are adapted less for coercing criminals than for irritating the upright; so that they cannot be maintained without great peril to the state." (*A Theological-Political Treatise, Chapter XX* in *The Chief Works of Spinoza*, Vol. I, trans. by R.H.M. Elwes, Dover Publications, 1951, pp. 261–262.)

According to Spinoza, a part of human nature is to yearn to exercise freedoms that have been denied, and, therefore, such prohibitions will always be resisted. A part of man's sovereignty is handed over to the state not to withdraw his liberty but to promote growth through freedom and to "lead men to live by, and to exercise, a free reason; they then may not waste their strength in hatred, anger and guile, nor act unfairly toward one another."

3. Locke

John Locke (1632-1704), the English philosopher called the founder of British empiricism, shared Spinoza's view that government was instituted to promote the interests of the governed. He defined the commonwealth as "a society of men constituted only for processing, preserving, and advancing their own civil interests." These civil interests include life, liberty, and property. The civil power of the government ("the magistrate") is confined to promoting "civil interests," and it cannot and ought not in any manner be extended to the salvation of souls.

In his *A Letter Concerning Toleration*, Locke appealed to the consciences of those who under the pretense of religion persecute, destroy, starve, and maim others with corporal punishment to make them Christians and procure their salvation. Nobody will ever believe, he maintained, that such torments can proceed from charity, love, and goodwill. God has never given to any man the authority to take care of the souls of others or to compel anyone to his religion. Such authority cannot be vested in the state even by the consent of the people, because no man can abandon the case of his own salvation. (For more on separation of civil government from the church, see my book *Equality, Tolerance, and Loyalty*, pp. 105-153.)

Locke's conception of a fiduciary relation between free individuals and rulers, with the government having the duties of the trustee and the community having the rights of the beneficiary, was appealing tó those who struggled for the preservation of the freedoms with which individuals are endowed by nature. These freedoms include freedom of speech and of the press.

4. Mill

Freedom, according to John Stuart Mill (1806-1873), one of the most famous English philosophers of the nineteenth century, comprises, first, liberty of conscience in the most comprehensive sense, including liberty of thought. It is impossible to separate from liberty of thought the cognate liberties of speech and the press, and absolute freedom of opinion on "all subjects, practical or speculative, scientific, moral, or theological." Second, freedom means the liberty to form our lives to suit our own tastes and characters, as long as what we do does not harm our fellowmen. Third, freedom involves the right to unite for any purpose not involving harm to others. (On a similar note, another famous English philosopher, Herbert Spencer (1820-1903), suggested that the formula of justice should be: "Every man is free to do that which he wills, provided he infringes not the equal freedom of any other man.")

In stressing that unrestrained freedom of discussion is essential to democracy, Mill wrote, "If all mankind minus one, were of one opinion, and only one person of the contrary opinion, mankind would be no more justified in silencing that one person than he, if he had the power, would be justified in silencing mankind." Mill argued that silencing the expression of an opinion is doing more harm to those who dissent from the opinion than those who hold it. "If the opinion is right, they are deprived of the opportunity of exchanging error for truth; if wrong, they lose . . . the clearer perception and livelier impression of truth, produced by its collision with error." ("On Liberty," in *Collected Works, Vol. XVIII, Essays on Politics and Society*, ed. by J.M. Robson, University of Toronto Press, 1977, p. 229.)

D. Censorship in America

The "great American experiment" in freedom and democracy was in many ways an attempt to put the great philosophers' theories of freedom and liberty into practical application. The fathers of our nation found the repression of thought and the pressure toward conformity in religion that both prevailed in Europe no longer tolerable. The idea of liberty grew gradually on our soil, but as it did, it became a beacon to all those around the world who dreamed of a life in which ideas and beliefs could be tested on their own merits, rather than being subject to the whims of official religious or political censors.

The freedom-loving settlers who came to this country to escape the religious intolerance and fanaticism they experienced in Europe were shocked, however, when they faced censorial theocracy in the new colonies as well—the natural result of government-established religions. The cruel persecutions they sometimes found were a repetition of the practices they had sought to leave behind in the Old World. Men and women of varied faiths who happened to be in a minority in a particular time or locality were persecuted because they persisted in worshipping God in the way their own consciences dictated.

The Massachusetts Bay Colony was dominated by clergymen of the Congregational Church, which in 1651 became the established church there. Quakers were persecuted and their books burned. Anne Hutchinson, an important religious leader of the New England colonies, after a trial before the General Court was sentenced to banishment for "traducing the ministers and their ministry." In 1635, Roger Williams was also banished from the Massachusetts Bay Colony for his "heretical opinions." Accompanied by others against whom the General Court had taken action because of their religious beliefs, he founded Rhode Island, to which England later confirmed the absolute liberty of conscience in religion and freedom of speech he had established.

1. The Trial of John Peter Zenger

A century later, the trial of John Peter Zenger, the American journalist who in 1734 was arrested and imprisoned on a charge of "scandalous, virulent, false and seditious reflections" in articles published in his *New York Weekly Journal*, helped to establish and advance the freedom of the press in the United States. The columns that appeared in Zenger's paper bitterly attacked Governor Cosby's administration in its quarrel with Rip Van Dam, a colonial politician and a leader in the struggle for popular rights. (Cosby, utterly devoid of statesmanship, ranked among New York's most unenlightened royal governors.)

In the trial, the famous lawyer Andrew Hamilton asserted that Zenger could not be imprisoned if the statements were proved true. The publisher's acquittal on the basis of the truth of the allegedly libelous articles was of special significance, since under the British common law a libel on the government was a crime and the truth of the statements was not a defense. The acquittal of Zenger was a humiliating defeat for the governor, who died about a year later. It was also a major milestone in the growth of the freedom of the press that would be officially proclaimed in the Bill of Rights a half-century later.

2. Thomas Jefferson and Freedom of the Press

Because of his role in drafting the Declaration of Independence, because of his extraordinary intellectual capacity, and because of his stout and repeated articulation of the principle of separation of church and state, the spirit of Thomas Jefferson has come to symbolize the American freedoms of press and religion. Jefferson believed fervently in liberty, and not only the United States but the entire world owes a great debt to his vision both of the rights and dignity of mankind and of the ability of the people to govern themselves. It should be stressed, however, that Jefferson believed in an *ordered* liberty. As strongly as he advocated freedom, he did not advocate license or an absolute liberty that takes no heed of the rights of others.

In the years before Jefferson became President, his rhetoric in defense of the freedom of the press carried him to the point of declaring that he preferred newspapers without a government to a government without newspapers. In a letter to a prominent Virginian, Edward Carrington, he wrote from Paris on January 16, 1787:

> "The people are the only censors of their governors. . . . The basis of our governments being the opinion of the people, the very first object should be

to keep that in sight; and were it left to me to decide whether we should have a government without newspapers or newspapers without a government, I should not hesitate a moment to prefer the latter. But I should mean that every man should receive these papers and be capable of reading them." (Phillips Russell, *Jefferson: Champion of the Free Mind*, Dodd, Mead & Company, 1956, p. 113.)

We may point out that Jefferson was a profound political philosopher but not always a consistent thinker. In his writings we may find other rhetorical excesses, to mention only his advocating the need for revolution every twenty years to nourish the tree of liberty and his declaring that every constitution and every law "naturally expires at the end of nineteen years." Such prophecies, if fulfilled, would have destroyed the American republic and the democracy rooted in our Constitution. Jefferson wrote the letter to Carrington when he was not yet in power. Some historians point out that when Jefferson became President, his attitude toward the press and its credibility changed.

In a February 19, 1803, letter to Governor Thomas McKean of Pennsylvania, he recognized the right of the states to exercise their power to punish seditious libels. To put an end to the Federalists' attack against freedom of the press by "pushing it's [*sic*] licentiousness & its lying to such degree of prostitution as to deprive it of all credit," Jefferson offered as a remedy a few wholesome prosecutions:

"This is a dangerous state of things, and the press ought to be restored to it's [*sic*] credibility if possible. . . . And I have therefore long thought that a few prosecutions of the most prominent offenders would have a wholesome effect in restoring the integrity of the presses. Not general prosecution, for that would look like persecution; but a selected one." (*The Writings of Thomas Jefferson*, Vol. VIII, ed. by Paul Leicester Ford, G.P. Putnam's Sons, 1899, pp. 218-219.)

As President of the United States he did not protest the prosecution of the Federalist editors of papers in Philadelphia (*Portfolio*) and New York (*The Wasp*) for crimes of seditiously libeling the United States and the President.

Is there inconsistency in Jefferson's ideas about freedom of the press? Not necessarily. In the history of the United States, we can hardly find a leader more committed to the idea of individual freedom than Thomas Jefferson. It was he who warned that our freedom will be lost if we are compelled to feel, think, and act in consonance with patterns dictated by those who by claiming a monopoly of rectitude and righteousness demand conformity and castigate any deviations from canons that they have established. On numerous occasions he conveyed to the nation his message that truth is discovered only when all ideas have an open field for fair consideration.

It was Jefferson who insisted that amendments to the Constitution be made to include the forty-five most important words describing individual freedom—the First Amendment:

> "Congress shall make no law respecting an establishment of religion, or prohibiting the free exercise thereof; or abridging the freedom of speech, or of the press; or the right of the people peaceably to assemble, and to petition the government for a redress of grievances."

So why would someone as committed to the principle of liberty as Jefferson call for "a few wholesome prosecutions"? The answer is that there is a limitation to individual freedom, namely, the freedom of others.

3. The Limits of Freedom of the Press

Although we strive for the greatest possible individual liberty from governmental authority, an individual's actions cannot adversely affect other members of society or the government elected by this society. Unbridled freedom may be in conflict with the principle of equality, which Thomas Paine attempted to explain by writing:

> "The principle of equality of right is quite simple. Every man can understand it, and it is by understanding his rights that he learns his duties; for where the rights of men are equal, every man must finally see the necessity of protecting the rights of others as the most effective security of his own."

The "necessity of protecting the rights of others" means that such a necessity may justify censorship—if not in the sense of a prior restraint of publication, at least in the sense of legal remedies after publication. Such a demand for legal responsibility on the part of those writing or publishing is not based on repressive power or prejudice. Rather, it is in the interest of providing a balance between the danger posed by license (which is the true nature of absolute freedom) and the individual liberty that is justly protected by the law.

Total freedom is the law of the jungle where only the fiercest, the strongest, and the most ruthless survive. Freedom is not absolute. It is justified only if in pursuing our own interest we do not deprive others of theirs or impede their efforts to obtain it. Freedom does not relieve the individual from his duty to contribute to the general interest of the society in which he lives or from his duty not to injure others by his conduct. This brings us to the need of stressing the justifiable aspects of censorship, which may be necessary to safeguard the performance of such duties.

Justifiable Forms of Censorship

The necessary forms of censorship have as their purpose the direction of human actions into constructive channels, thus enhancing the interest in the welfare of our society. Such limitations are diametrically different from the repressive, prohibitive censorship that characterizes governmental action to restrain free circulation of books and newspapers or free exchange of ideas and thoughts.

We shall limit our discussion on positive forms of censorship to two of the enduring justifications of such censorship: national safety and interference with the administration of justice (trial by newspapers and the media).

A. National Safety

The right of free speech is one of the most cherished policies of a freedom-loving society. An untrammeled press is and always will be a vital source of public information. The question, however, arises, Is there a constitutional obligation to extend this right to individuals who advocate the violent overthrow of the government duly elected by the people or who promote teachings that tend to subvert the government and to hinder it in the performance of its duties? History shows us that such utterances may kindle a spark that, while smoldering for a time, may break open with sudden violence into a sweeping and destructive fire. The United States Supreme Court has taken the position that the state cannot reasonably be required to measure the danger from such utterance "in the nice balance of a jeweler's scale." The state is not acting arbitrarily or unreasonably when it takes measures necessary to extinguish this spark without waiting until it blazes into a conflagration.

On June 15, 1917, two months after the declaration of war on Germany, Congress passed the Espionage Act. The act called for imprisonment of up to twenty years and fines up to $10,000 for anyone who obstructed recruiting or enlistment; conveyed false statements with the intent to interfere with the operation of the military or naval forces; or attempted to cause insubordination, mutiny, or disloyalty in the armed forces. One of the few cases ever tried under this act was that against Charles T. Schenck and Elizabeth Baer, defendants who were convicted for directly and dangerously interfering with conscription by mailing circulars to the draftees, describing the draft as an unconstitutional arrangement in the interest of the capitalists of Wall Street and urging the recipients to assert their constitutional rights.

The Supreme Court unanimously affirmed Schenck's conviction, and Justice Oliver Wendell Holmes enunciated the "clear and present danger" standard, which sought to serve the cause of a free press at the same time that it protected the society from "substantive evils":

> "The question in every case is whether the words are used in such circumstances and are of such a nature as to create a clear and present danger that they will bring about the substantive evils that Congress has a right to prevent. It is a question of proximity and degree. When a nation is at war many things that might be said in time of peace are

such a hindrance to its effort that their utterance will not be endured so long as men fight and no Court could regard them as protected by any constitutional right." (*Schenck v. United States*, 249 U.S. 47 [1919].)

A few days after the *Schenck* decision, on March 10, 1919, the Supreme Court, guided by its own precedent, sustained a conviction against Eugene Debs for making a speech obstructing and attempting to obstruct the recruiting and enlistment service of the United States. Before his speech, Debs also approved the Socialist antiwar proclamation adopted at St. Louis in April 1917. The proclamation recommended opposition to the war through all means and suggested that capitalism was the cause of war and that our entrance into the war against Germany was instigated by the predatory capitalists of the United States. It also alleged that the war of the United States against Germany could not "be justified even on the plea that it is a war in defense of American rights or American honor." (*Debs v. United States*, 249 U.S. 211 [1919].) President Wilson refused to approve the recommendation of the Justice Department for commutation of Debs's sentence, effective February 12, 1922.

Using as its yardstick the clear and present danger standard defined above, the Court rejected the "reasonable tendency" test that previously had been its standard (I shall return later to this topic). In so doing, the Court ruled that the "substantive evil" must be extremely serious and the degree of imminence extremely high before any utterances can be punished. The tension between the freedom of press and the concept of a clear and present danger that may bring about substantive evil is illustrated by two later dissenting opinions written by

Justice Holmes with the concurrence of Justice Louis D. Brandeis. (For a fuller discussion of these two cases, see my book *Equality, Tolerance, and Loyalty*, pp. 141–145.)

The lack of a consensus over the definition of what might constitute a clear and present danger became evident in the case of *Abrams v. United States* (250 U.S. 616, 617, 40 S.Ct. 17 [1919]). There the question arose of whether the *Schenck* opinion offers a serviceable test. During World War I, the defendants in the *Abrams* case were charged with conspiring to unlawfully utter, print, write, and publish "disloyal, scurrilous and abusive language about the form of government of the United States," to "incite, provoke and encourage resistance to the United States in said war," and to "incite and advocate curtailment of production of things and products necessary and essential to the prosecution of the war." After denouncing President Wilson as a hypocrite and a coward and assailing our government in general, the defendants appealed to the "workers" of this country to arise and put down by force the government of the United States as a "capitalistic enemy."

The articles of the *Abrams* defendants contained a definite threat "to create so great a disturbance that the autocrats of America shall be compelled to keep their armies at home, and not be able to spare any for Russia." There was also a threat of armed rebellion. "If they will use arms against the Russian people to enforce their standard of order, so will we use arms, and they shall never see the ruin of the Russian Revolution."

The Supreme Court affirmed the judgment of the District Court for the Southern District of New York convicting the defendants of conspiring to violate provisions of the Espionage Act. The plain purpose of their criminal conduct, stated the Court, was "to excite, at the supreme crisis of war, disaffection, sedition, riots, and, they hoped, revolution in this country for the purpose of embarrassing and if possible defeating the military plans of the government in Europe."

Justice Holmes in his dissent argued that the principle of the right to free speech is always the same, even against charges peculiar to war. "It is only the present danger of immediate evil or an intent to bring it about that warrants Congress in setting a limit to the expression of opinion where private rights are not concerned. . . . Now nobody can suppose that the surreptitious publishing of a silly leaflet by an unknown man, without more, would present any immediate danger that its opinions would hinder the success of the government arms or have any appreciable tendency to do so." (250 U.S. 616, 628, 40 S.Ct. 17, 21 [1919].)

This lack of consensus over the direction of public policy and over a definition of the limits of free speech appeared also in the case of *Gitlow v. People of the State of New York*. Benjamin Gitlow was indicted for the statutory crime of criminal anarchy as defined by the New York Penal Code. The judgment was affirmed by the Court of Appeals. The defendant, a member of the Left Wing Section of the Socialist Party, advocated in a published *Manifesto* the destruction of the state and the establishment of the dictatorship of the proletariat by "organizing the industrial proletariat into militant Socialist unions and at the earliest opportunity through mass strike and force and violence, if necessary, compelling the government to cease to function, and then through a proletarian dictatorship, taking charge of and appropriating all property. . . ." (268 U.S. 652, 662, 45 S.Ct. 625, 628 [1925].)

The Supreme Court affirmed the judgment of the Court of Appeals that held that the *Manifesto* "advocated the overthrow of the government by violence, or by unlawful means." It is a fundamental principle, stated the Supreme Court, that the freedom of speech and of the press "does not confer an absolute right to speak or publish, without responsibility, whatever one may choose, or an unrestricted and unbridled license that gives immunity for every possible use of language and prevents the punishment of those who abuse this freedom."

Freedom of speech and of the press does not protect publications promoting the overthrow of the government by force or teachings that tend to subvert the government or to hinder it in the performance of its duties. The state, according to the Supreme Court, is the primary judge of regulations required in the interest of public safety and welfare, and its statutes may be declared unconstitutional only when they are arbitrary and unreasonable.

Justice Holmes, in his dissenting opinion, agreed that the test sanctioned by the full Court in *Schenck v. United States* applied in this case. In Holmes's judgment, however, "if in the long run the beliefs expressed in proletarian dictatorship are destined to be accepted by the dominant forces of the community, the only meaning of free speech is that they should be given their chance and have their way." (*Gitlow v. People of the State of New York*, 268 U.S. 652, 673, 45 S.Ct. 625, 632 [1925].) Furthermore, the publication of the manifesto, he stated, did not attempt to induce an uprising against the government at once but at some indefinite time in the future, and therefore, it was too remote from possible consequences to meet the test.

Obviously, when writing his dissenting opinions in the *Abrams* and *Gitlow* cases in 1919 and 1925, respectively, Justice Holmes could not foresee how deep the human depravity brought on by communism and Nazism would be. Nor was he able to give consideration to this depravity when he made his distinction between mere advocacy of a forcible overthrow of the government and actually preparing a group for violent action or steeling it to such action.

Thirty years after the *Schenck* opinion, the Supreme Court had to make a distinction between mere dissatisfaction or anger that induces unrest and serious, substantive evil that rises above unrest. Stressing the merits of free speech, the Court stated that the function of free speech

> "is to invite dispute. It may indeed best serve its high purposes when it induces a condition of unrest, creates dissatisfaction with conditions as they are, or even stirs people in anger. . . . That is why freedom of speech, though not absolute . . . is nevertheless protected against censorship or punishment, unless shown likely to produce a *clear and present danger of serious substantive evil that rises far above public inconvenience, annoyance, or unrest.*" (*Terminello v. City of Chicago*, 337 U.S. 1, 4, 69 S.Ct. 894, 896 [1949]. Emphasis added.)

The clear and present danger concept, criticized for being too vague and for conflicting with the Bill of Rights, underwent expansion in *Dennis v. United States*. Under the Smith Act of 1940, Eugene Dennis had been convicted with ten other communist leaders for advocating and teaching the violent and forcible overthrow of the government. Speaking for the Court of Appeals for the Second Circuit, which upheld the conviction, Judge Learned Hand offered a new test for sedition cases that would substitute for the clear and present danger test. He wrote, "In each case Courts must ask whether the gravity of the 'evil,' discounted by its improbability, justified such invasion of free speech as is necessary to avoid the danger." In other words, there is no need for the government to wait for the imminence of the danger and/or its arrival in order to take preventive action.

The United States Supreme Court, following the revised version of the Holmes clear and present danger opinion, sustained the conviction. Chief Justice Vinson, upholding the constitutionality of the Smith Act, wrote:

> "An analysis of the leading cases in this Court which have involved direct limitations on speech ... will demonstrate that both the majority of the Court and the dissenters in particular cases have recognized that this is not an unlimited, unqualified right, but that the social value of speech must, on occasion, be subordinated to other values and considerations. . . .
>
> "Certainly an attempt to overthrow the Government by force, even though doomed from the outset because of inadequate numbers or power of the revolutionists, is a sufficient evil for Congress to prevent. . . . We agree that the standard as defined is not a neat mathematical formulary. Like all verbalizations it is subject to criticism on the score of indefinitiveness." (*Dennis v. United States*, 341 U.S. 494 [1951].)

Justices Black and Douglas dissented, claiming that the laws suppressing freedom of speech and the press on the basis of Congress's notions of mere "reasonableness" water down the First Amendment.

1. The Pentagon Papers

Closer to our times, the publication of the Pentagon Papers became another chapter in the history of the struggle between censorship for the sake of national safety and the public's right to information. In 1969, Daniel Ellsberg, an employee of the Rand Corporation, was accorded access by Defense Department officials to a large compilation of documents that came to be known as the Pentagon Papers. These were massive documentations and analyses of the American involvement in Southeast Asia. Ellsberg had been a marine and a military consultant for both the Defense Department and the State Department but had become disenchanted with the war effort. Under the influence of Vietnam War protestor Anthony J. Russo, Jr., Ellsberg copied the entire contents of the documents, which were so secret they had not even officially been logged into the Rand security files.

Two years later, Ellsberg's opposition to the war had grown to the point that he decided to publish the papers in his possession. *The New York Times* began their publication in June 1971, and immediately the Nixon administration took steps to try to block further installments from appearing. The government took the matter to court, and Judge Murray I. Gurfein, who had been on the bench only a few days, issued a temporary restraining order. Then stories based on the Pentagon Papers began appearing in newspapers all over the country.

On June 30, the Supreme Court finally ruled, six to three, that prior restraint of publication of the papers was illegal. All nine Justices wrote opinions in the case.

Six were in favor of lifting the injunction; three offered support for the government position but couched their opinion in various ways. As one of the dissenters, Justice John Marshall Harlan, pointed out, "I cannot believe that the doctrine prohibiting prior restraints reaches to the point of preventing courts from maintaining the status quo long enough to act responsibly in matters of such national importance as those involved here." Since no opinion by a single Justice commanded a majority, the Court issued its ruling in an unsigned order that stated, "Any system of prior restraints of expression comes to this court bearing a heavy presumption against its constitutional validity." (*New York Times v. United States*, 403 U.S. 713 [1971].) The Court's ruling left open the question of whether the newspapers and Ellsberg could subsequently be successfully prosecuted on the grounds that the government's classification policy was valid and could be enforced through lawful criminal proceedings.

Meanwhile the Justice Department had secured an indictment against Ellsberg for copying the papers. A trial began in 1972, but shortly after the jury was sworn in, the trial was suspended by order of Supreme Court Justice William O. Douglas, Jr., on the grounds that an inadmissible wiretap by the government might have tainted the defense's right to a fair trial. The jury was kept intact for more than five months—an unprecedented length of time for a suspended trial—but was finally disbanded under pressure from the Circuit Court.

Finally, on May 11, 1973, Judge William Matthew Byrne, Jr., granted a mistrial and dismissed the case against Ellsberg and Russo on the grounds that the government had egregiously overstepped good legal procedure in its investigations. (In addition to the wiretaps and the retrieval of information from the Central

Intelligence Agency, E. Howard Hunt and G. Gordon Liddy had burglarized the office of Ellsberg's psychiatrist, Dr. Lewis Fielding, in search of information that might be damaging to Ellsberg.)

In Judge Byrne's declaration of the mistrial, he said, "The charges against these defendants raise serious factual and legal issues that I would certainly prefer to have litigated to completion." (Peter Schrag, *Test of Loyalty: Daniel Ellsberg and the Rituals of Secret Government*, Simon and Schuster, 1974, p. 355.) But the improprieties of the government's investigation had made it impossible to hear the case against Ellsberg fairly. Thus a crucial modern test case concerning the validity and enforceability of the government's classification policy and its right to secrecy in matters of national security failed to materialize.

The unanswered question remained of whether the government has the final authority in deciding whether a certain piece of information might, when revealed to the public, endanger our national security. Is the press bound by a decision by the government to classify a piece of information when the press claims that the publication of the information can cause no danger to our national interest and that the government's decision is unsound or frivolous?

2. Voluntary Domestic Censorship

During World War I (and later during World War II), a system of voluntary domestic censorship, with restraints self-imposed by the press, was established in the United States. Under pressure from the press, Congress, in the Espionage Act that passed on June 15, 1917, rejected the so-called censorship provision that would have given the President the right to determine what kind of information might be helpful to the enemy and prevent its publication. The defeated provision would have inflicted penalties, including imprisonment, for the publication of such proscribed information. The press for the most part applauded the Espionage Act (passed without such a provision) and called for the enforcement of the laws relating to treason or conspiracy against the government.

The Espionage Act was followed by the 1918 Sedition Act, which extended the offenses specified by the earlier statute to include "unpatriotic" utterances and writings and publications attacking the government, military uniforms, or the flag. With few exceptions—mainly from socialist newspapers—the press supported the Sedition Act as well. The press regarded it as another measure for rooting out the anti-American and pro-German utterances of disloyal citizens or enemy aliens, not as an attempt to restrict the liberty of expression guaranteed by the First Amendment.

The Supreme Court decisions also reflected the political climate of that time in stressing the merits of the war and in handing down convictions for public expressions unfavorable to the conduct of the war. The climactic judicial test came in the cases described above that were tried before the Supreme Court under the 1917 Espionage Act (*Debs, Schenck*) and under the 1918 Sedition Act (*Abrams*). The Sedition Act was repealed in 1921.

As a historical note, it may be pointed out that the first Alien and Sedition Acts had been passed by Congress long before, in June and July 1798. President John Adams made no use of the law empowering him to expel dangerous aliens, so the Alien law was never enforced. It expired unused two years after its enactment. Not so with the Sedition Act. The arrests of editors who criticized the government helped to unite the Republicans in opposition. The Federalist Party suffered a defeat in the subsequent presidential elections, and when Jefferson took office in 1801, he pardoned all who were prisoners under the Sedition Act.

In the 1940s, the press was supportive of the Smith Act, which had been passed by the Congress in 1940 and prohibited advocacy of the violent overthrow of the government. It was invoked only twice during World War II (once against eighteen members of the Socialist Party accused of conspiracy to violate the law, and the second time in a case against twenty-eight pro-Nazis that was later dismissed). With the anticommunist climate that characterized the period of the Cold War with the Soviet Union, a series of subsequent prosecutions did take place under the Smith Act. The *Dennis* case (described above) gained a favorable reaction from the press for its claim that freedom of speech is restricted only to legitimate purposes. Senator Joseph McCarthy, in the early stages of his "crusade" against communist infiltration into governmental agencies, found support from a number of newspapers. Only when some of the leading newspapers became targets of McCarthy's accusations did they denounce his tactics of name-calling never substantiated by legitimate evidence.

During the Vietnam War, the news media did not hesitate to point out the contradictions between official governmental reports and the actual happenings on the battlefront. The graphic presentation of the sufferings of the local population and of wounded Americans augmented the skepticism about, if not indeed the resentment toward, war in general and the Vietnam war in particular.

During the invasions of Grenada and Panama, reporters were not allowed to cover the action; and during the Persian Gulf war, the government expanded and made more rigid the ground rules for the behavior of journalists by imposing unprecedented restrictions on where reporters could go and what they could show of combat. They were not allowed to take pictures of casualties or of wounded soldiers, for instance. They were also required to pass tests of physical fitness never introduced in previous U.S. wars in order to demonstrate that the reporters were fit enough to cope with the blazing desert sun and thus would not slow down the troops in the battle zone. In addition, the number of reporters covering combat at any given time was limited. Correspondents were required to submit their reports to military censors, and the rules of appeal from the censors' decisions were complex enough to delay publication long enough to deprive the reports of relevancy.

The press, perturbed by the distrust between the Pentagon and the media, appealed for the suspension of some of the rules on the grounds that the patriotism, honor, and good judgment of the journalists could be relied on. I recall that one of the popular television personalities reporting from Saudi Arabia complained about the imposed restrictions by assuring the viewers that "although I know where our armed forces are located, I have enough good judgment not to report it." This brings back the question considered earlier of who has the right to decide whether a certain piece of information might endanger our national safety—the government or the press?

In answering this question, we fully realize the reasons why we distrust censors on the general principle of *Quis custodiet ipsos custodes?* ("Who guards the guardians?")

and fear their actions. We also realize that even in a democracy, government officers are subject to human weakness, irrationality, and delusions that might affect the objectivity of their decisions to classify certain pieces of information as secret. Winston Churchill once said that democracy is the worst form of government ever devised by men—except for all the other forms. Or, to quote Thomas Jefferson, "Sometimes it is said that a man cannot be trusted with the government of himself. Can he, then, be trusted with the government of others? Or have we found angels in the form of kings to govern him?"

We have found no angels in the form of kings and by no stretch of the imagination do we attribute infallibility to government officials. As Spinoza had pointed out, the weakness of democracy is its tendency to put mediocrity into power. He believed that the only remedy would be to limit office to individuals of "trained skill."

The inherent power to establish a classification system and to protect it belongs to the government. When our government officials apply censorship in violation of the First Amendment, legal avenues can be pursued to reverse their decisions and ultimately to replace the government with other elected officials who will honor our constitutional rights of freedom of the press and free exchange of ideas. There is no recourse, however, against poor judgment on the part of reporters who publish classified documents that had officially been placed into security files, except subsequent prosecution through criminal proceedings. Less harm will be done to our national safety if a journalist publishes such documents only after having ascertained through available legal avenues that the classification policy or a particular classification decision had in fact been legally invalid.

Through our representative form of government, which permits debate and the free exchange of ideas, government becomes responsive to the will of the people. Through such a free exchange of ideas, the wisdom of political decisions—including classification decisions— can be carefully evaluated by every member of a democratic community who has the right to vote in a free and fair election. The First Amendment is one of our fundamental rights, but in accordance with the "will of the people" the right to free speech may be outweighed by public interest that prevents the publication of information that could serve our enemies, especially in time of war.

3. Secret Diplomacy

I would suggest one exception—namely, secret diplomacy—from the principle I have outlined calling for the validity and enforceability of the government's classification decisions as long as a document has not been declassified through due process. History gives ample evidence that secret diplomacy, along with imperialistic ambitions, has often plunged the world into war. Some of us still have vivid memories of World War II, which followed the secret Soviet-Nazi pact dividing Europe into spheres of influence.

A number of philosophers and statesmen have pointed out the danger of secret diplomacy. Among modern philosophers, we can point to one of the greatest, Spinoza, who wrote in his *Tractatus Politicus*:

> "[I]t is far better for the right counsels of a dominion to be known to its enemies, than for the evil secrets of tyrants to be concealed from the citizens. They who can treat secretly of the affairs of a

dominion have it absolutely under their authority; and as they plot against the enemy in time of war, so do they against the citizens in time of peace. . . . But the perpetual refrain of those who lust after absolute dominion is, that it is to the essential interest of the commonwealth that its business be secretly transacted. . . ." (Chapter 7, in *Chief Works of Benedict Spinoza*, Vol. I, trans. by R.H.M. Elwes, Dover Publications, 1951, p. 342.)

In his famous "Fourteen Point" speech, delivered on January 8, 1918, before a joint session of Congress, President Wilson outlined a program for world peace. In this program, which he described as "the only possible" one for peace, he declared that secret diplomacy had to be abolished. The first of the Fourteen Points calls for "open covenants of peace, openly arrived at, after which there shall be no private international undertaking of any kind, but diplomacy shall proceed always frankly and in the public view." As history shows us, truth may be withheld from disclosure, on one occasion or on many. But over the course of time we find that the truth is rediscovered, along with the full realization of the tragic consequences caused by secret diplomacy conducted by governments confident in their own infallibility.

B. Interference With the Fair and Orderly Administration of Justice

The First Amendment prohibits any law abridging freedom of speech or of the press. These freedoms, however, are not so absolute that they permit utterances calculated to intimidate the fair course of justice. Free speech and the right to a fair trial—those choicest privileges of the American people—do not conflict with each other, and both deserve the broadest scope that can be accepted in a free society. Freedom of the press and freedom of speech, which are safeguards essential in restraining those who wield power, may become self-destructive when they intrude into the living process of fair adjudication or disturb the calm course of the administration of justice.

The courts have the power to protect themselves from coercion and intimidation and from disturbances in the courtroom by taking appropriate measures, including the common-law procedure of punishing on the grounds of contempt. One of these measures is the power to punish individuals or organizations for publications made outside the court if they tend to interfere with the fair and orderly administration of justice in a pending case.

Until 1941, in federal courts the basis for administering punishment for a publication on grounds of contempt was its "inherent tendency" or "reasonable tendency" to interfere with the orderly administration of justice. In the 1941 case of *Bridges v. State of California*, the Supreme Court decided that such "tendencies" are not enough to justify restriction of free expression. (314 U.S. 252 [1941].)

As a replacement for the reasonable tendency standard, in order to safeguard the historical constitutional meaning of the freedom of the press, the Court offered the practical guidance described above in *Schenck v. United States*. Instead of tendencies, the Court recommended as an appropriate guide a standard of clear and present danger in determining the constitutionality of restrictions upon freedom of expression. The clear and present danger principle requires "that the substantive evil must be extremely serious and the degree of imminence extremely high before utterances can be punished."

1. A "Carnival" Atmosphere

One of the most notable Supreme Court cases dealing with the tension between the freedom of the press and a defendant's right to a fair trial was *Sheppard v. Maxwell.* Dr. Samuel H. Sheppard in 1955 had been accused of murdering his wife, Marilyn, in a suburb of Cleveland, Ohio. The local and national press took a great interest in the case, and from the beginning the chief prosecutor and police investigators were quoted in the newspapers and on television as saying that Dr. Sheppard was uncooperative, that he refused to take a lie-detector test, and so on. Various other allegations about romantic involvements on the part of Sheppard (who had not yet been formally accused) also surfaced in the press.

Less than three weeks after the murder, editorial statements attacking Sheppard began appearing even on the front page of the local newspaper. The coroner's inquest was broadcast live. Sheppard was subsequently indicted and came up for trial two weeks before the November general election, in which both the prosecutor and the presiding judge were candidates.

The publicity surrounding the trial was overwhelming. The names and addresses of the seventy-five veniremen called for possible service on the jury were published in the newspaper. A table for reporters was set up *inside the bar of the courtroom,* right next to the jurors' box, and the jurors themselves were constantly exposed to the news media. Both newsrooms for the printed media and broadcasting facilities for the radio were installed within the courtroom itself. In a debate staged by, and broadcast live over, the local radio, the participants—newspaper reporters—asserted that Sheppard had conceded his guilt by hiring a prominent criminal lawyer.

Many of the charges printed or broadcast were never heard from the witness stand—for instance, that Sheppard was a perjurer and a "barefaced liar"; that his wife had characterized him as a "Jekyll-Hyde"; and, finally, that a woman convict claimed that Sheppard was the father of her illegitimate child. To summarize, the newspapers devoted particular attention to the material incriminating Sheppard and frequently drew unwarranted inferences from testimony.

When the case finally came on appeal to the Supreme Court in 1966, it was reversed with only one dissenting vote. The majority opinion, written by Justice Tom Clark, agreed that "every court that has considered this case, save the court that tried it, has deplored the manner in which the news media inflamed and prejudiced the public." (384 U.S. 333, 356, 86 S.Ct. Reporter 1507, 1519 [1966].) The Supreme Court noted that the trial court had ample means with which to regulate prejudicial publicity, such as stricter rules governing the use of the courtroom by newsmen, insulation of the witnesses from reporters, and control of the release of leads, information, and gossip to the press by police officers, witnesses, and the counsel of both sides.

In the event that prejudicial treatment of the facts by the press might have taken place despite these precautions and disciplines, the courts would always have the option of a change of venue or a delay until the glare of publicity had subsided. Although the trial court was reversed because it had failed to impose control over the statements made to the news media by counsel, witnesses, the coroner, and police officers, Justice Clark's opinion shows a reluctance to suggest court actions aimed directly at newspapers and broadcasting companies.

2. Intimidation

The cases of *Bridges v. State of California* and *Times-Mirror Co. v. Superior Court of California, in and for Los Angeles County*, considered together by the Supreme Court, arose as a result of California state court convictions of labor leader Harry Bridges and of the publisher and the editor of the *Los Angeles Times*. These two cases concerning different parties were related by the issue of the proper scope of the First Amendment in safeguarding free speech and a free press. (314 U.S. 252 [1941].)

The Times-Mirror Company, the publisher of the *Los Angeles Times*, and L.D. Hotchkiss, the newspaper's managing editor, were cited for contempt for publishing three editorials. The most serious offense, according to state courts of California, was the editorial entitled "Probation for Gorillas?" which vigorously denounced two members of labor unions who had previously been found guilty of assaulting nonunion truck drivers. This editorial closed with the warning that the judge on the case, A.A. Scott, would make a serious mistake if he granted probation to the two convicted members of the labor union. "This community," observed the editorial, "needs the example of their assignment to the jute mill."

The state courts took the position that, if the court acted contrary to the recommendation contained in the editorial and granted probation, it might well expect adverse criticism in the columns of the *Los Angeles Times*. This basis for punishing the publication for contempt was the publication's inherent tendency and its reasonable tendency to interfere with the orderly administration of justice in an action before the court for consideration.

The Supreme Court of the United States did not find that an editorial of this kind actually threatened to obstruct the administration of justice. The expected adverse criticism in the event probations were granted could come only after the disposition of the pending case, and judges are not beyond criticism. To regard such a threat of criticism "as in itself a substantial influence upon the course of justice," stated the Supreme Court, "would be to impute to judges a lack of firmness, wisdom, or honor, which we cannot accept as a major premise."

In the *Bridges* case, the trial involved a dispute between two labor unions. The officers of the local San Pedro Harbor union sought to transfer the allegiance of the local away from the International Longshoremen's Association (ILA), an affiliate of the American Federation of Labor (AFL), and tie it to the International Longshoremen's and Warehousemen's Union (ILWU), an affiliate of the Committee for Industrial Organization (CIO). The Superior Court enjoined the officers from working on behalf of the ILWU and appointed a receiver to conduct the affairs of the local as an affiliate of the AFL by taking charge of the outstanding bargaining agreement and of its hiring hall—the physical mainstay of such a union.

While a motion for a new trial (filed by the ILWU, the defendants in the injunction) was pending, Harry Bridges, the president of the ILWU and also the West Coast director of the CIO, sent a telegram to the Secretary of Labor that found its way into the metropolitan newspapers of California. The telegram described the judge's opinion as "outrageous"; it pointed out that any attempt to enforce it would tie up the port of Los Angeles and involve the entire Pacific coast. It concluded with the announcement that the ILWU "does not intend to allow state courts to override the majority vote of members in choosing its officers and representatives and to override the National Labor Relations Board."

The state courts of California regarded the telegram as a threat that an attempt to enforce the decision would result in a strike that could tie up the entire Pacific coast and in the 11,000 longshoremen belonging to the ILWU not abiding by the court's decision. The Supreme Court of the United States took the position that, since it was not claimed that such a strike would have been in violation of the lower court's decision or of the law of California, on no construction could "the telegram be taken as a threat either by Bridges or the union to follow an illegal course of action." Moreover, in sending the message to the Secretary of Labor, Bridges was exercising the right of petition to a duly accredited representative of the United States government, a right protected by the First Amendment.

The Supreme Court of the United States did not find that Bridges' utterance "tended" to interfere with or obstruct justice. In other words, the Court reversed the state court decision because the telegram and its publication did not "create a clear and present danger" that would bring about a "substantive evil," which according to the *Schenck* decision would justify a restriction upon freedom of speech or the press.

Justice Black delivered the opinion of the Court. That opinion provoked a strong dissent from Justice Frankfurter, concurred with by the Chief Justice, Justice Roberts, and Justice Byrnes. The dissenting opinion questioned the advisibility of denying the application of the reasonable tendency test—called "this age-old formulation of the prohibition against interference with impartial adjudication"—and its replacement by the clear and present danger test, which justifies curbing an utterance only when it is warranted by the substantive evil to be prevented.

Following the *Bridges* case, the Supreme Court, in its highly protective attitude toward the press, held in a series of cases that the evidence in each was insufficient to show a clear and present danger that might bring about a substantive evil in the administration of justice. (Some examples are *Pennekamp v. Florida*, 328 U.S. 331 [1946]; *Craig v. Harney*, 331 U.S. 367 [1947]; and *Wood v. Georgia*, 370 U.S. 375 [1962].) What is the substantive evil in question? The answer is, interference with impartial adjudication. The two kinds of test that we have been discussing (reasonable tendency and clear and present danger) are dealing, therefore, with the same kind of issue. Both kinds of test require the exercise of good judgment in their application. The distinction between the two tests, established in the *Schenck* decision, is that the clear and present danger test is linked with the "question of proximity and degree." This suggested criterion seems to be, at best, very vague.

As I pointed out in my discussion of interference with the orderly administration of justice, the clear and present danger test has been abandoned in many other fields relating to limitations on the freedom of speech and of the press. (See the case of *Dennis v. United States*, described above.) The recent history of judicial administration shows that controlling prejudicial publicity (as suggested by Justice Clark) is more consistent with the traditional American preference for an uncensored press. The rule that must guide the courts in determining whether there is interference with impartial adjudication—and guide as well all human conduct—is the rule of reason. This rule demands conditions providing for calm and orderly court decisions and the condemnation of coercive utterances directed toward pending proceedings.

3. Criticism of Judges

In making this argument, we must stress the word "pending." Court decisions are not above criticism. Justice Brewer in an address delivered on Lincoln Day, 1898, stated:

> "It is a mistake to suppose that the Supreme Court is either honored or helped by being spoken of as beyond criticism. On the contrary, the life and character of its Justices should be the objects of constant watchfulness by all, and its judgement subject to free criticism. The time is past in the history of the world when any living man or body of men can be set on a pedestal and decorated with a halo. True, many criticisms may be, like their authors, void of good taste, but better all sorts of criticism than no criticism at all. The moving waters are full of life and health; only in the still waters is stagnation and death."

Our courts have the power to cite as contemptuous those publications that would tend to interfere with the administration of justice only when a case is pending. Once the case is closed, courts are subject to the same criticism as other institutions. Decisions of the court are not the fundamental law of the land. Only the involved parties are obligated to obey them. The Constitution, not the decisions of the court, is the constitutive law of the land. Criticism of the court decisions often stimulates a healthy discussion about the meaning of a particular constitutional provision. Judges are not exempt from common fallibilities and frailties. Constructive criticism expressed with candor reminds judges of their limitations and their public responsibility.

As long as a case is pending, the decisions reached by the court should be influenced only by evidence and arguments before it, not by outside influences, whether of private talk or publication. As the Supreme Court pointed out in the *Bridges* case, legal trials "are not like elections, to be won through the use of the meeting-hall, the radio, and the newspaper." Measures to prevent trial by the news media and the carnival atmosphere that dominated the *Sheppard* case do not contradict the traditional, well-established constitutional preference for an uncensored press. Such measures are not an abridgment of free speech or freedom of the press. They are indispensable to protect the public from coercive intrusions from outside the judicial process—intrusions that might hamper its calm, impartial, and orderly administration of justice.

Ordered Liberty

Censorship, as I mentioned in the beginning of this lecture, has appeared in all stages of history. In this lecture I have discussed at length only two reasons for censorship: protecting the safety of our nation and preventing interference with the orderly administration of justice. Court decisions and administrative decrees, however, have also tried to clarify the meaning of other abuses of the freedom of expression, such as obscenity, pornography, blasphemy, sedition, libel, slander, and malicious representation. Unfortunately, the history of censorship shows that on numerous occasions it has been hypocritically applied in the name of preserving a certain moral order established by the authority in power. This arbitrary kind of censorship has been applied not only to the media but also within the realm of the arts and other forms of expression, to mention only personal dress. History also shows that moral traditions—the common sense of the community, its sense of decency, propriety, and respect for established ideas and institutions—vary with the times and geography. A variety of causes brings about changes reflecting the forces molding the concepts of morality governing a society.

The most laudable of such changes are those that result from the search for truth. The results of this search for truth may be extinguished temporarily by oppressive forces, but they will continue to reappear in more favorable circumstances until they prevail over the attempts to suppress them. In our political system, our independent courts have been vested with the responsibility to resist every encroachment by these oppressive forces against the liberties stipulated in our Constitution and the Bill of Rights.

Our rights to freedom of speech and of the press must be exercised in conformity with the need to preserve public order, a responsibility vested in the government. Above all rights rises our duty—our responsibility to the community and our concern for its welfare. This responsibility calls for an accommodation between the rights of the individual and the preservation of social order. Since the spirit of our Constitution is one of ordered liberty, not of license, we must learn to reach such an accommodation. The line between liberty and order should be drawn by means of an empirical process that responds to the sensible claims of citizens to their rights and to the responsibility of government to maintain a free but orderly democratic society.